WISDOM
from Above

WISDOM
from Above

D R . B E T T Y R . P R I C E

FAITH ONE
PUBLISHING
Los Angeles, California

WISDOM FROM ABOVE, Vol. 1 by Dr. Betty R. Price
Published by Faith One Publishing
7901 S. Vermont Avenue
Los Angeles, CA 90044

This book is produced and distributed by Creation House, a part of Strang Communications, www.creationhouse.com.

Unless otherwise noted, all Scripture quotations are from the New King James Version of the Bible. Copyright © 1979, 1980, 1982 by Thomas Nelson, Inc., publishers. Used by permission.

Definitions are from *Merriam-Webster's Collegiate Dictionary*, 10th edition (Springfield, MA: Merriam-Webster, 1993), 62–66, 71–76.

Cover design by Justin Evans

Library of Congress Control Number: 2007931870
International Standard Book Number: 987-1-59979-241-5

First Edition

07 08 09 10 11 — 987654321
Printed in the United States of America

CONTENTS

INTRODUCTION

I N JAMES 3:17, THE BIBLE tells us: "the wisdom that is from above is first pure, then peaceable, gentle, willing to yield, full of mercy and good fruits, without partiality and without hypocrisy."

For a number of years now, the ladies of Crenshaw Christian Center have gathered together for our annual luncheon, which we call "Wisdom From Above." I really look forward to having this time with the women away from the church. Not only do we have a chance to break bread together but I also have the opportunity to share with them what I believe God has laid upon my heart concerning the challenges facing us today and the solutions to those challenges, which really is the Word of God. This book was developed from notes I prepared for those women's meetings. At the root of many of the problems I address each year is the fact that most people don't know the Word or how to apply it to their lives to help them be successful in their daily living. The Word has brought me from poverty to wealth, from sickness to health, from discouragement to a life of peace and joy. The Bible teaches that God is no respecter of persons, and what He has done for me He will do for anyone who is willing to learn and obey His Word.

Jesus said in John 10:10: "The thief [speaking about Satan] does not come except to steal, and to kill, and to destroy. I have come that they may have life, and that they may have it more abundantly." God wants the body of Christ to live in abundance. That is why He gave us His written Word—the Bible—so that we can know what He has provided for us through His Son, Jesus Christ, the Living Word.

Since being in the ministry with my husband, my desire has always been to help believers, especially women, know their rights in Christ, to encourage them to reach for the highest call of God, and to live the victorious, overcoming life. Volume one of this book was written to share with you how to walk in God's Spirit and to draw on His heavenly wisdom to make it through this life. Volume two will further discuss how to grow in God's wisdom and understand just how important God's wisdom is in our lives. I encourage you to know that the Bible, the Book, is not just to be read and put aside. But it is *life* to all who discover its truths—and treat it as such. If you do, you will find that abundant and blessed life God has for you.

—DR. BETTY R. PRICE

Chapter 1

Walking in
the Spirit

Walk in the Spirit, and you shall not fulfill
the lust of the flesh.

—GALATIANS 5:16

THE BODY OF CHRIST IS in constant warfare with
a tricky enemy who refuses to give up. It is a spiritual battle that gets hotter as time goes on. The spirit
world exists right along with our natural world, and
when we are moving for God, we become target practice for the devil. It doesn't mean that we are necessarily
doing anything wrong when things come against us; it
is just the way Satan plays his game. If you are doing
something you have no business doing and you know
it, you need to stop whatever it is, because you are only
opening yourself up to satanic attacks.

When cancer attacked my body, a lot of people who
knew me wondered why. Some even said, "It is not

fair; you live so pure." You don't get healed because you are good and live pure. You get healed because you believe and act on the Word, and that includes staying free from sin. People don't really understand that. Christians take a lot of persecution from the world, as well as from the devil, but God honors His Word if we will believe it.

I raised my children in the fear (reverence) of God and taught them to act on the Word, so they were able to go through life's situations and come out OK. My husband and I put them in the hands of the Lord and taught them His Word. They knew that when we were not with them, God was with them. I'm not saying that it was always easy, because you have to constantly take a stand against the wiles of the enemy. But when the Bible says to have faith in God, that is what you have to do, no matter what you are faced with.

A lot of people don't understand how faith works. They take the faith message all out of proportion. They don't understand that when you say you believe something has taken place before you see it, healing for example, you are saying it by faith. They think that means you don't take medicine or you don't go to the doctor. Some Christian leaders have even given the faith message a bad name because they don't really understand how faith operates. Faith healing does not mean that you do not take medicine or go to the doctor, because you might need to go to the doctor and take medicine while you make a stand to receive your healing. People have done a lot of things foolishly by following what they think rather than following the Bible.

When I found out I had cancer, we had just returned from a television crusade in Houston, Texas. In fact, while I was there in Houston, I had asked a doctor who was a member of our church and had gone to the crusade with us to come to our hotel room to have a look at my leg because it was so swollen and was becoming very painful. She said I should see a doctor as soon as possible when we returned to Los Angeles. As soon as we got off the plane, Fred called another doctor who was also a member of our church and asked him to meet us at our daughter Angela's house since he lived close to her and not too far from the airport. Dr. Taylor came over and did some tests on my leg, but since it was the Memorial Day weekend he could not get the results from the lab right away. He didn't find anything obviously wrong from the tests he took, but he said he did not like the way my leg looked.

In the meantime, Dr. Taylor called another doctor who lived next door to us and asked him if he could come to our home and look at my leg. This doctor took a look at my leg and said to Fred, "Your wife needs to go to the hospital immediately." He called and made the necessary arrangements. We thought that it was just a sprain or a strained muscle and I would be home within a day or so. I actually stayed a week in the hospital having tests done before they found out what was wrong with me. At any rate, I never did get anxious, worried, or fearful. I was at peace the whole time; I had learned to walk in the Spirit.[1]

After several days of taking tests, some very painful (but God was with me all the way), the doctors came and told us the bad news. The MRI revealed a tumor in my pelvic area, but because of its location, major surgery would have to be done to get a biopsy of it. I was scheduled for surgery the next day, which was Monday. That Tuesday morning, Dr. Taylor came and gave us the really bad news. The tumor was a malignant cancer that had vital nerve endings and muscle attached to it. Therefore, surgery to remove it was impossible. The recommended cure was chemotherapy and radiation. Fred, of course, was devastated. He could not believe it. Even with all of the pain, I never felt any unrest or fear. I was always in peace. I was learning to walk in the Spirit. The biopsy surgery left me in a great deal of pain, and I could hardly talk, let alone move. I wondered how I would ever live through the pain because pain was everywhere. But I said, "I have to trust God. I know He is with me in this, and nothing is too hard for Him."

Angela was with her father when he was told about my situation. She handled the news pretty well, but Cheryl, another of our daughters, was just devastated. She would come visit me, but though she couldn't stay at home, she was just not any good in the hospital either. She would spend the whole time crying. You would have thought I was dead. I ended up praying for them. I was learning what it means to walk in the Spirit. At any rate, after I was released from the hospital, I told Fred that I had decided that I was going to stand and believe God for my complete healing and not take the chemo or radiation. That was my decision. God never told me to do this. He did give me a specific Word, but He did not tell me not to take the chemo or radiation. The first night I was in the hospital, I felt the Lord's presence so strongly that I knew He had come into my room, and I heard in my spirit, "'This sickness is not unto death, but for the glory of God, that the Son of God may be glorified through it'" (John 11:4).

So instead of dwelling on thoughts of death, I kept my thoughts on God's Word. That is why I want to exhort you not to take the Word for granted. If I had not had twenty years of Word in me at that time, I don't believe I would be here today. When you hear the word *cancer,* fear will raise its ugly head. It's only natural, but you don't allow the fear to take hold. I believe fear a lot of times is what actually kills people, so I would not allow myself to be fearful.

Because a lot of Christians don't agree with what Fred has taught so much on faith and healing, some people probably wished I would die so that they could prove that faith healing does not work. But healing is true, even if I had not received my healing. Regardless of the outcome, it is still true because healing is not based on someone's experience; it is based on God's Word. You need the Word when negative thoughts come. When you are sick and not feeling good is not the time to start looking up healing scriptures. As fast as those negative thoughts would come, I would counteract them with the Word. You have to have the scriptures already in your spirit. Second Corinthians 10:5 tells us what to do with negative thoughts:

> Casting down arguments and every high thing that exalts itself against the knowledge of God, bringing every thought into captivity to the obedience of Christ.

So when Satan comes and tells you, "You are going to die," you have to know that the Bible says with Jesus' stripes you were healed. (See Isaiah 53:5.) Your confes-

sion is, "I believe I'm healed." You have to know also
that Mark 11:24 says:

> Whatever things you ask when you pray, believe
> that you receive them, and you will have them.

Your confession is, "I believe I receive because the
Bible says if I believe I receive, I will have." It is so
sad, but this is where many Christians miss it. They
can't understand that they have to believe they receive
before they see it, and then they shall have. They want
to see it before they believe it, and faith just does not
work that way. I wish it did, but it doesn't. That is why
you have to take a stand and believe that you have what
you asked for.

Hebrews 11:1 says:

> Now faith is the substance of things hoped for,
> the evidence of things not seen.

Faith is the evidence that you have what you have
prayed for. I would tell myself, "I don't see it now, but by
faith I have it. Faith is the tangibility of my healing." Most
people want to go by sight and by the way they feel. It
is difficult for them to understand how faith works. But
I had the faith principles so ingrained in me that when
the attack on my body came, I knew how to stand and

not let fear come in. Now your situation may not be a healing one; maybe it's a financial problem or a husband or wife problem or children problems. Whatever the problem, you can apply the same faith principles.

Second Corinthians 4:18 tells us:

> While we do not look at the things which are seen, but at the things which are not seen. For the things which are seen are temporary, but the things which are not seen are eternal.

The things we are going through are just temporary. My illness was temporary. The things of God are eternal. God's Word says that we are healed by Jesus' stripes, and that is eternal. However, it is up to us to believe it and receive it.

Second Corinthians 5:1 says:

> For we know that if our earthly house, this tent, is destroyed, we have a building from God, a house not made with hands, eternal in the heavens.

You have to know where you stand with God so Satan can't come in and put fear on you about death and dying. I told the doctors when they came with the bad news that I was not afraid of the surgery. They really didn't want me to have the surgery, but there was no other way of getting to that tumor. I said to them,

"I'm not afraid of the surgery; I'm not even afraid to die." I can tell you this right now, I am not afraid to die. The Apostle Paul says that to be with the Lord is far better, but I know it is needful for me to stay here to continue to do the work God has committed to my husband and to me as my husband's helper. Also, God should have examples of people who are willing to take His Word and stand on it and let the world know that Satan is not ruling God's children.

God has given us great and precious promises, and it is up to us to believe these promises. He cannot believe them for us. There are multitudes of scriptures that tell us God is with us when we are going through trying times. We just need to meditate on and confess these promises when situations come against us. For instance, the Twenty-third Psalm should be a part of every Christian's confession. These verses are not just there for us to read, but to apply to our daily life, because they take into consideration our every need.

> The Lord is my shepherd; I shall not want. He makes me to lie down in green pastures; He leads me beside the still waters. He restores my soul; He leads me in the paths of righteousness For His name's sake. Yea, though I walk through the valley of the shadow of death, I will fear no evil.
> —PSALM 23:1–4

It is up to you not to fear evil. You have to do it. Your will is involved. It doesn't matter what you feel like; you have to be determined that you will not fear. When I was waiting for the manifestation of my healing, I took all these verses to heart. Everything that came my way and everything that Satan tried to throw against me, I would use the Word against it.

I hear people say, "Well, you can do something wrong and not even know it." God has that covered:

> Bless the Lord, O my soul; And all that is within me, bless His Holy name! Bless the Lord, O my soul; And forget not all His benefits: Who forgives all your iniquities, Who heals all your diseases [that includes cancer or anything else that attacks you], Who redeems your life from destruction, Who crowns you with lovingkindness and tender mercies.
>
> —PSALM 103:1–4

If I am believing God, I can't believe what the devil is trying to put on me.

Jeremiah 17:7–8 tell us:

> Blessed is the man who trusts in the Lord; And whose hope is the Lord. For he shall be like a tree planted by the waters, Which spreads out its roots by the river, And he will not fear when heat

comes. But its leaf will be green, And will not be anxious in the year of drought. Nor cease from yielding fruit.

Heat represents darkness and wickedness. We are going to have the heat, but we don't have to have the fear. Why? Because God is with us and He is our protection. To "not be anxious" means not to be worried or overly concerned, even though "drought" will come. No matter what the devil throws at us, he can't stop us. Now this does not mean that we are going to be free of problems just because we are Christians. We are in the world, and Satan is the prince of this world. But if we are walking in the Word, we will be better protected because God honors His Word.

I get comfort from the Word, so I don't look at what is happening around me. It should be the same with you. In any kind of circumstance you might find yourself, God will take you right through it and give you the strength to overcome whatever it is you may be going through.

Proverbs 3:5–6 says:

Trust in the Lord with all your heart, And lean not on your own understanding; In all your ways acknowledge Him, And He shall direct your path.

God didn't give us these verses because they sound pretty. He wants us to apply them to our everyday lives.

In Isaiah 41:10, God says:

> Fear not, for I am with you; Be not dismayed, for I am your God. I will strengthen you, yes, I will help you. I will uphold you with My righteous right hand.

God really is concerned about us, and He wants the best for us. He does not want us constantly going through problems and frustrations. If this is where you are, do what Psalm 37:4 says:

> Delight yourself also in the Lord, And He shall give you the desires of your heart.

Stop worrying about so many things around you. Always worrying and wondering. Some women are always wondering about: When am I going to get a husband? When is this going to come to pass? I been waiting for a husband for years; when is it ever going to happen? God has the right time and the right one for you. Stop worrying about getting a husband and get busy serving God. You surely don't want to become involved with someone who is not right for you. Do you? Then you'll really have problems.

First Corinthians 10:13 says:

> No temptation has overtaken you except such as
> is common to man; but God is faithful who will
> not allow you to be tempted beyond what you are
> able, but with the temptation will also make the
> way of escape, that you may be able to bear it.

I know that God is faithful. You have to believe that
and act like the Word is true, which it is. No matter
what you are facing, you will come through with the
Lord's help. I did. He was with me through a very rough
ordeal, but I am still here today because God honored
His Word and brought me out into a wealthy place.

CHAPTER 2

WALKING IN THE FLESH

For the flesh lusts against the Spirit, and the
Spirit against the flesh.

—GALATIANS 5:17

IN DEUTERONOMY 30:19, GOD TOLD the people:
"I have set before you life and death, blessing and
cursing; therefore choose life, that both you and your
descendents may live." I used this scripture for my
healing. Even though it was first spoken to the Israelites,
it is still just as true today as it was back then. When
that attack came upon my body, I did not believe God
would have told me to choose life and then let me die.
You have to believe that God is with you and not go by
how you feel or by what you see. When you go by your
feelings, you are walking in the flesh.

That is why it is so important to understand what
faith is all about. Some people walk in faith for a while,

but because something doesn't happen right away, they give up: "Well I believed God for this and I didn't get it. Then I believed God for that, and I didn't get that." A lot of times people are believing for things that their faith has not been built up for. In other words, they are over-extending their faith and believing beyond their ability to sustain their faith. That is one of the reasons my husband teaches that we should start using our faith on the little things in life first and build up to bigger things. As our faith grows we can believe for bigger and bigger things.

Hebrews 11:6 tells us that without faith, it is impossible to please God. In the beginning of our faith walk, Fred and I were just so thrilled to know that believing God was a way we could please Him. We didn't know all the benefits that would come to us as a result of our walking in faith.

Through faith and love for God, we raised our children without any real problems. They grew up like other kids their ages, having to face the dope scene, premarital sex, smoking, drinking, and all the other junk. But they kept themselves free from all that because they knew God was real, and we lived the right way before them. Our daughter Angela used to say, "We had the fear of daddy in us. I just believed God would have given daddy a word of knowledge if we were doing anything wrong." You may say, "I didn't know about God until later and my children had already gotten off into some bad things." Well, start where you are, determining to make a change, and as you sincerely turn to God and ask for and rely on His help, He will bring you through whatever you are going through. Cast the care of your children, husband, or whatever your family situation is upon the Lord. I share this over and over again. Someone asked me one time (almost in amazement), "Does God really want us to do that? Yes, He does or He would not have told us in 1 Peter 5:7 to do it.

The Bible says in Philippians 4:6: "Be anxious for nothing, but in everything by prayer and supplication, with thanksgiving let your requests be made known to God." If you do that, you will have what the next verse says: "and the peace of God, which surpasses all understanding, will guard your heart and minds through Christ Jesus" (v. 7). When you sincerely do that, you will sense God's peace, and that's when you know you have truly cast the care upon the Lord. You have to train yourself not to worry, especially if you have a tendency to worry. I came out of a family of worriers, but I trained myself over the years not to worry. The benefits are great.

We should not allow ourselves to look at our circumstances if we want to stay in the Spirit and not walk in the flesh when we are believing God for something. A good example of this is found in the book of Romans where it talks about God's promise to Abraham about having a son. If you know the recorded event of Abraham and Sarah, you remember that Sarah, Abraham's wife, was barren, but God told Abraham that he would be the father of many nations.

Romans 4:17:

> (As it is written, "I have made you a father of many nations") in the presence of Him whom he believed—God, who gives life to the dead and calls those things which do not exist as though they did.

That is what faith does; it calls those things that are not as though they were. It does not call those things that are as though they were not. It may seem like a play on words, but actually that is the way God has worked all through the Bible.

Romans 4:18:

> Who contrary to hope, in hope believed, so that he became the father of many nations, according to what was spoken, "So shall your descendents be."

At that time, Abraham was seventy-five years old, and his wife was sixty-five years old. She had been barren all her life and now was past the age of reproduction. And here is God telling them they were going to have a son. They could hardly believe it. When you read this fourth chapter, it looks like the minute God said that to Abraham, he believed it right away and it happened. It actually took twenty-five years for this promise to come to pass. It took him twenty-five years to work up his faith to produce the promise. Abraham was actually one hundred years old when Isaac was born, which made Sarah ninety. It says, "Who contrary to hope, believed in hope." Abraham believed God's promise. He had to have believed it in order for the promise to come to pass.

Romans 4:19–21:

> And not being weak in faith, he did not consider his own body, already dead (since he was about a hundred years old), and the deadness of Sarah's womb. He did not waver at the promise of God through unbelief, but was strengthened in faith, giving glory to God, and being fully convinced that what He had promised He was also able to perform.

At first, Abraham didn't believe what God said. If he had, he never would have had his son Ishmael from his wife's servant, Hagar, as an attempt on their part to bring the promise to pass. It took them some time of walking with God and seeing His faithfulness for their faith to rise to the point where they believed God's promise.

It is the same faith principle that Abraham used that we can use today for whatever we believe God for—whether it's a child, money, husband, wife, or healing. The principle is the same: you have to believe you receive before you see it. We have a promise in the Bible from God for whatever we need. When you understand how faith works, you won't have a battle with your flesh; you won't give into fear, and you won't give into negative thinking.

There are pastors, preachers, and church leaders who say they believe in healing. But then when someone who is close to them dies, they start backing off faith right away, saying, "Well, I used to believe God healed, but now this happened to my friend, and my friend was so good. He did everything right, so since this happened to him, it couldn't be God's will to heal everybody."

This is not good thinking. You don't know what your friend believed or did not believe, not that you are supposed to know about what he is doing or not doing because it is none of your business. But we should not put God down and say it is not His will to heal because someone you know did not get healed.

Some of these unbelieving believers will use an account like Job's and say, "Well, God did allow those things to happen to Job." Yes, God allowed it because Job allowed those things to happen. Faith and fear cannot operate together. If you read the third chapter of Job, you will see where he allowed fear to come in.

> For the thing I greatly feared has come upon me.
> —JOB 3:25

Then there are those who say things like, "Well, God says that Job was perfect before Him." Yes, Job was an upright man, but that does not mean he was perfect in all ways because no one is perfect (except Jesus, of course). We don't always do everything right. Most of us don't eat right, or at least I didn't before I got sick. We do some things just out of bad habits. I used to drink twelve cups of coffee a day. That is bad—very bad—and what made it even worse was that I didn't drink water because I didn't like water. So is there any wonder we have things that happen to our bodies? We need to work on the things we do that are wrong. Yes, you may have a perfect heart towards God, morally speaking, but then you may sit down to eat a steak and get tired of chewing it and swallow it, which will cause you digestive problems. We need to correct all those little things before we start saying things like, "That faith stuff doesn't work; healing does not work." It is not that God doesn't heal; He actually has done everything He is going to do. He has put the laws of good health in motion; however, it is up to us to work those laws.

Hebrews 4:1–2 says:

> Therefore since a promise remains of entering His rest, let us fear lest any of you seem to have come short of it. [This was talking about the children of Israel.] For indeed the gospel was preached to us as well as to them, but the word which they heard did not profit them, not being mixed with faith in those who heard it. [This is talking about the Christians.]

God had given the Israelites the Promised Land, but they had to go in and possess it. He could not do that for them. He had already told them that everywhere the sole of their feet tread, He had given (past tense) them that land (Deut. 11:24). But there were some unbelievers in the crowd who said that they could not take the land because there were "giants" in the land, and they could not possess it, even though God had told them the land was theirs. Because they would not go and take the land, God could do nothing, so they wandered in the wilderness for forty years until all the unbelievers had died.

Sadly, that is the way many Christians are today. Many of us don't really believe God, or rather don't know how to believe. We don't trust God enough to know that if we do our part, He will do His. We have to possess our promised land. We can't be like the children of Israel and say, "There are giants in the land, and we are as grasshoppers in our own sight" (Num. 13:33, author's paraphrase). Even though God had given them the land, they would not take possession of it. They allowed their ungodly thinking to stop them, and that is what happens when we allow our flesh to control our thinking. God never said we would not have any challenges in this life. In fact, He said that our afflictions would be many, but that He would deliver us out of them all. (See Psalm 34:19). When I was under attack, I stood on God's promises of healing. I just believed that nothing really could happen to me because God was with me. I don't care how bad the pain was or how bad I felt, I would say constantly, "Lord I know you are with me." You have to make up your mind. That is what you have to do if you want to win in life.

No matter how bad I felt, I went on all the crusades and ministered to the ladies there. No one knew how sick I was feeling. I never really looked sick, even though I heard someone say, "My, she looks frail," because I had lost quite a bit of weight. I didn't care what people said; I was acting by faith because I believed that according to God's Word I was healed. Satan opposed me in many ways. Sometimes it was like the devil was a real person, and he would sit at the end of my bed or bathtub talking to me: "You are a fool. Nobody in the world who feels like you would go out and do what you are doing." I would ignore what I was hearing, and the Lord always gave me the strength to go on and do all the things that I needed to do as a helpmeet to my husband.

I had missed church for the first three months of the attack. When I started going back to church, I would sit in my office because at that time my feet were swelling a lot. I would sit in my office until it was time for the choir to sing, just before Fred taught the Word, and then I would join the rest of the congregation. I would come out then because it was hard for me to sit three hours at one time, but I was there. I didn't like missing church, especially not hearing the Word, because every word I heard helped to increase my faith. You cannot allow Satan to intimidate you. You have to stand your ground, and you can't do that if you are giving into the flesh.

I quoted a part of the Ninety-first Psalm during my daily prayer time: "No evil shall befall me, and no plague shall come nigh my dwelling" (v. 10, author's paraphrase). I would quote it to the devil and tell him, "Devil, you hear that? No evil shall befall me and no plague shall come nigh my dwelling." This is why I believed that none of that ugly cancer could stay in my body. I believed all those beautiful scriptures I learned and was applying to my life. They brought me through and kept me from looking at the negative circumstances. As I did this, God gave me the strength to be an overcomer. His faithfulness has caused me to have even more of a reverence for Him and His Word. The desire of my heart, for not only the corporate body of believers at Crenshaw Christian Center but for the body of Christ everywhere, is that we would so dedicate ourselves to the Lord that when the world sees us, they will see Jesus. We can do this by not giving in to the flesh. When we walk in the Spirit, that is living in the spirit world. The spirit world is more real than this visible world. God is in the spirit world. In fact, God is a Spirit and He made this visible and material world out of the spirit world. So that has to mean that the spirit world is more real, which means God is more real.

I have a little message that my brother sent me during my attack. And if you are going through something, you can apply this to your life, too. This is a true story about a United States senator named Clinton Anderson.[1]

At twenty-one years old, Anderson had begun a promising career as a newspaper writer and was planning to get married when he contracted tuberculosis (TB). That was in the days when TB was incurable. He was sent to New Mexico and confined to bed in a sanatorium. His condition became hopeless, and the doctors wired his father to come within five days if he wanted to see his son alive. Anderson said he seriously considered taking is own life. One day he noticed somebody standing at the side of his bed. He looked up to see an old TB patient named Joe Mias. What Joe Mias said saved Anderson's life. Mias said, "Remember son, what you got will never kill you if you keep it in your chest. [Tuberculosis is a disease that most often affects the respiratory system.] But if you let it get up here," tapping his head, "it's fatal. Worrying kills more people than TB ever did." Anderson was so inspired by this little message that he showed signs of improvement almost immediately. He got stronger, began writing articles and poems, and later joined the hospital newspaper staff. He passed Joe Mias' warning against letting physical illness become a "mental illness" on to every patient he could. He was determined at this point to keep the illness in the flesh and not let it rule his mind. The story has a happy ending: Anderson remained in New Mexico, serving as a United States senator from New Mexico and earning a nationwide reputation.

This is what we have to do as Christians. Joe Mias said, "Keep it in the body—not in the mind." We know that means, keep negative thoughts out of our spirits. This was how I felt. When I went through the attack, my body was in much pain, and I hated to see my husband and children hurting to see me go through the ordeal. But it did not touch my spirit or my mind.

Everyone can be strong in the Spirit. It is a matter of making up your mind to spend time with the Lord through prayer and study of His Word. You can't be strong if you don't spend time in the Word or time praying in the Spirit. So many people don't understand about being filled with the Holy Spirit and praying in other tongues. They think it's something weird. But that is a tool God has given us to build our spirit man up. When you pray in the Spirit, you build up your inner man. First Corinthians 14 says that "he who speaks in [an unknown] tongue edifies himself (v. 4). You are building up your inner man so that your inner man can exercise control over the outer man. That way, whatever happens you will act from your spirit man and not from your outer man. And as you do that you are, "Building yourself up on your most holy faith, praying in the Holy Spirit" (Jude 20). So when you are attacked with a negative situation, you will know what to do because you will know it in your spirit. God ministers to your spirit, but He can't pray in the Spirit for you. He can't get into the Word for you. He can't read the Word for you, and He can't possess the land for you. But He will confirm His Word in your life if you will commit your life to Him.

Don't take God's Word for granted. Don't take His wonderful gift of the Holy Spirit for granted; don't even take your salvation for granted. The Bible tells us in James 1:2, "Count it all joy when you fall into various trials." Notice, it says when and not if you fall. That means Satan is going to come against you, but if you are "prayed up" and you have spent quality time with the Lord, you can defeat him every time. Know that nothing is too hard for God.

When I got to my last chemotherapy session, I thought I could not make another day. When I had my last radiation session, I thought I could not go another day. But God saw me through all that. He is faithful, and He will continue to see me through, no matter what I have to face. He will do the same for you.

CHAPTER 3

WALKING IN THE BLESSINGS OF GOD

The blessing of the Lord makes one rich.

—PROVERBS 10:22

THE BLESSINGS OF GOD ARE available to every believer, and yet we see so many Christians go without their needs being met. Why are there so many in the body of Christ not receiving from God when He has given us scripture after scripture telling us that we are overcomers and victorious? What is lacking? Why aren't we overcoming? Why can't Christians receive what Jesus paid for with His blood and life to give us? First John 5:4 says:

> For whatever [whoever] is born of God overcomes the world. And this is the victory that has overcome the world—our faith.

John 8:31–32 tell us:

> Then Jesus said to those Jews who believed Him, "If you abide in My word, you are My disciples indeed. And you shall know the truth, and the truth shall make you free."

Why are there so many people bound with all types of problems? Why aren't they experiencing the freedom Jesus promised? Obviously, they are not abiding in the Word.

> Stand fast therefore in the liberty by which Christ has made us free
>
> —GALATIANS 5:1

> Now thanks be to God who always leads us in triumph in Christ.
>
> —2 CORINTHIANS 2:14

These are just a few of the scriptures that tell us we are overcomers. So why aren't more of us walking in victory? In ministering and counseling with people, one of the key things I find is that most believers don't really understand what Jesus has done for them. They don't truly know Him in a personal way. They don't realize that though they can't see Him physically, He really is with them. This is where faith comes in. Many believers won't even receive the Holy Spirit so that they can pray with other tongues. This is the language of their recreated spirit, which they received when they accepted the gift of the Holy Spirit. We need to pray in tongues every day in order to develop our spirit man. When your spirit man is strong, you will believe Jesus is real, because one of the jobs of the Holy Spirit is to make Jesus real to the believer. When Jesus is real to you, you will not go by how you feel, but by what the Bible says.

Unforgiveness Can Stop Your Faith

One of the things that a lot of Christians have to deal with is the problem of unforgiveness. They don't know how to forgive themselves, nor do they know how to forgive others. Many times, people have made mistakes in their pasts—maybe they had a child out of wedlock, had an abortion, or committed adultery or fornication—and they don't know how to forgive themselves for that. Some people were abused as children, and they carry the memory of that abuse around with them all their adult lives, not knowing how to get rid of that memory. They can't seem to accept that God truly loves them and wants them to be free of whatever is holding them in bondage. They might say, "Well,

I forgive the person," or, "I forgive myself." But they don't feel like they are forgiving or forgiven because they have an enemy who is constantly reminding them of the things they did or the things that happened to them in the past.

The Apostle Paul tells us in Philippians 3:13–14:

> Forgetting those things which are behind and reaching forward to those things which are ahead, I press toward the goal for the prize of the upward call of God in Christ Jesus.

To live in the blessings of God, you are going to have to forget whatever happened to you in the past: Be it a bad marriage, a bad relationship, abuse, or anything else bad that happened to you. In other words, you are going to have to forgive and forget, and it doesn't matter how bad the problem was or how bad it hurt. God knows how much it hurt and how bad it was, but He told you to forgive and forget. He wants you to forgive yourself so that you can walk in freedom. If you don't forgive yourself and carry around a lot of guilt and resentment, you only open the door for Satan's attack. A lot of sickness comes from that kind of stuff. You may say, "Well, that's hard to do. It is always before me; it's always on my mind." You can forget because you're a child of God, and you have His ability. You can forget the same way He forgets. How does God forget? He wills to. In Hebrews 8:12 God says:

> For I will be merciful to their unrighteousness, and their sins and their lawless deeds I will remember no more.

If God doesn't remember, He doesn't want you to remember either. And the way you do that is to make it an act of your will: "I *will* remember," or, "I *will not* remember." A lot of times we want to remember certain bad situations because we want to be sad, having people feeling sorry for us all the time. But that doesn't really help in the long run. It is much better to do what God does: forgive and forget. If you don't, you are going to keep dwelling on that and you will be miserable for the rest of your life. And when you get older, having carried all that junk inside you all that time, different things can begin to go wrong in your body. Mainly, it will be because you did not do what God said do by forgiving and forgetting.

God Is the Only One We Can't Make It Without

A lot of women act as though they can't make it without a man. The only one you can't make it without is the Lord. There are so many women who put up with all kinds of junk from men. I am not against men because I have been married to a man for well over fifty years, but some men—too many in fact—do treat women badly.

God has called us to peace, especially in our marriages. If you are in a marital situation where you are always fighting and struggling, if you are going to stay in the marriage, you are going to have to make up your mind that you will (1) cast the care of your spouse on the Lord and believe that God will take care of the situation and (2) live in peace. Of course, it goes without saying that physical abuse is not even a consideration. No one should stay in a situation where they are being beat up. I have heard some women say that they can't take verbal or mental abuse either. Personally, I think you can, that is if you are strong in the Lord, because you are supposed to be dead to yourself. Even though I think I could take it, you know what you can take, so the decision has to be yours. The main thing is not to let the abuse get to you. You must know how much you can take and not let someone kill you. It is your responsibility to decide what you can and will put up with. If you don't take action, you can end up making yourself sick on top of the effects of the abuse. God will not hold you responsible for the abuse, but because your body is the temple of the Holy Spirit He does want you to treat it with respect.

I'm thinking about some pastors' wives I know. Some of them really put up with a lot of junk. They do so mainly because their lives are so public and everyone is watching them all the time. One pastor's wife whose husband left her with three kids and went off with somebody else ended up in a mental hospital. Do you think I'm going to let some man put me in a mental hospital? I don't think so. And God can't do anything about it because He has given us the responsibility to take care of ourselves. In this situation you need to tell that man to go somewhere and jump in a lake. Then let God bring you somebody else who is worthy of you. But don't let a man (or woman, as the case may be) keep you so worried, depressed, and stressed that you can't even function.

Again, our wills are involved. There are a lot of things that can bring stress upon you—job, home, children, and relationships—but you are going to have to learn how to deal with them. Apparently, we are able to do it, because God's Word says so. The only time we can't is when we are doing a lot of things we shouldn't be doing.

It Is Important to Raise Children in the Word

When you have children, it is important to have the Word as your guide. We raised our children in the fear of God, so we really didn't have a lot of problems. God's Word works. We used it on our daughters and they came through those difficult teen years without any problems: no drugs, drinking, smoking, or sex. They came up godly in the midst of the drug scene. We put the fear of God in them. You as a parent must live right before your children and let them see God in your life, and then they'll know that God is real.

As many of you know, in our old age and quite to our surprise, we had a son. I had two grown girls and an eleven-and-a-half-year-old girl, and then we had this boy. Actually, our first child was a boy. He was killed by a car while crossing the street when he was only eight years old. His name was Frederick K. C. Price, III, after his father and grandfather. Frederick is our second son, and we named him Frederick Price. Many people call him Price, Jr. although he is not really the junior. When Freddie came along, Fred and I thought we were through having children, but God had other plans for us. Before he was born, we received a prophecy that the child I was carrying would be a boy and he would help my husband in the ministry, just as our first son would have done, had Satan not stolen his life. The prophecy came to pass, and Frederick, an assistant pastor at Crenshaw Christian Center, is proving to be a wonderful blessing to his father and me, the ministry, and most of all to the Lord.

We raised him the same way we raised our daughters, because based on the Word of God we believe boys should be sexually pure as well as girls. We made sure he stayed free from drugs, smoking, and alcohol, just as we did our daughters. There are all kinds of risqué programs on television, and if the parents are not watchful, kids will look at them. We didn't just go and turn the television off and tell him he could not look at television if we saw him watching them. We would say to him, "We don't do those things in this house. No sex until you are married." We kept that message before him. Fred and I would talk to him about the things he had to face out in the world and the pitfalls Satan has for young men. I would tell him all the time, "Don't get yourself off in a corner with some girl by yourself and start getting your feelings all bothered." You have to tell your children what is out there and then expect God to back you up. When they are tempted to get in certain situations, God will bring what you have taught them to their remembrance if you keep it before them. Sometimes it brings stress. It costs something to raise godly children because they want to do all the things that they see other kids do. Some parents are afraid to chastise their kids, thinking they are going to run away. Give those kids to God and go on and do what is right. They will appreciate it later.

First Peter 5:7 tells us:

> Casting all your care upon Him, for He cares for you.

A lot of Christians think those are just beautiful words to read and they don't apply them personally, but you can apply the Word of God personally in your life. That is what we did in raising our children.

Living the Single Life

A lot of times single people are not walking in God's blessing because they feel they can't enjoy their Christian life since they are not married and the world is always pulling at them. God knows what you need. We counsel married couples who are having a lot of problems in their marriages. We also counsel a lot of single women who are wondering if God has forgotten them and when they are going to get a husband. Some even get stressed out over this. So we have a married woman who is having a conflict with her husband and wishing she could get rid of him, and then we have the single woman who wishes she had him. The married woman says, "Well, you can have mine." And the single woman says, "Oh, how handsome he is; I want him." But she doesn't know what is on the inside of him.

I know it can be difficult being single, even though I didn't have to stay single for a long time. I married when I was nineteen, not too long out of high school. However, I can still relate to what single people go through. But more importantly, God can relate. He is your Father, and He wants the best for you. He tells you, "Delight yourself also in the Lord, and He shall give you the desires of your heart" (Ps. 37:4).

I know a lady who didn't get married until she was fifty-four years old because she was believing God for a certain kind of man to marry. Some of you are probably thinking, "I hope it doesn't take me until I'm fifty-four." When I met her, she was seventy years old, but she looked forty because she never carried around all the stress and worry that a lot of women go through—both married and single. The man she married was a widower and a little younger than she. He already had beautiful children, so they became her children. Just think, she had children and she didn't have to go through carrying and raising them. She said her husband was wealthy, a Christian, and he treated her wonderfully. You see, it's never too late for God. You just have to get your mind off of looking for a mate and spend time doing things as unto the Lord.

So many times women let men cause them to commit fornication or adultery. Then the guys end up leaving them and the women are in worse shape than they were before. You can't believe a man just because he tells you things you want to hear. Tell him to marry you first. It is just that simple. You need to do what God says, and you will reap the benefits. If you don't, then you will be the one to pay the price later.

Power of Prayer

Many believers are concerned about unsaved family members. Pray for your family. I pray for my family all the time. I believe they are all saved, filled with the Holy Spirit, healed, and living godly lives. Even if they are not, that is my confession of faith for them. I thank God for sending forth laborers to minister to them so they will know about Him and that they will be delivered from whatever is keeping them in bondage. You have to learn to do that for your family. You have to be diligent and disciplined to do it. After all, you may be the only one who is praying for them. Satan doesn't want you to pray or get into the Word, but you have to be disciplined to do it.

Prayer is so very important. You might think your job and the other things you are involved in are what is sustaining you. But you have to know that it is God who is totally behind any blessings you get. It is up to you to do your part, and God will do His. I'm a living witness. I came from real poverty to where I am now, and it was rough. But God brought us out of every situation. Third John 2 says:

> Beloved, I pray that you may prosper in all things and be in health, just as your soul prospers.

That is God's desire for all of His children, and He will provide you with whatever you need. But you have to take it a step at a time. He knows whether you are "shucking and jiving." He knows whether you are just serving Him for the blessings or whether you are serving Him because you love Him and you want the very best of God in your life. I want my life to glorify and honor God. That is all I care about. I tell my kids the same thing: "This family is set aside to serve God." Like Joshua said, "Choose for yourselves this day whom you will serve.... But as for me and my house, we will serve the Lord" (Josh. 24:15).

I pray for my children daily that they will give God their best and they will have His best. I pray for my grandchildren that they will have sensitive spirits and alert minds, and they will live for God all the days of their lives. The Christian life is a wonderful life. I can't express to you the peace that will be in your life when you walk in the will and blessings of God. And no matter what attacks you, God will see you through every situation you are faced with. Unfortunately, most Christians don't have the patience it takes to wait on God. You have to have patience with the things of God that is why Hebrews 10:23 tells us to:

> Hold fast the confession of our hope without wavering, for He who promised is faithful.

If you really believe that, you'll hold fast until you receive the promised blessing.

Some people might think, "Well, what happened to you?" God is not telling us a lie. If we are not receiving the blessings of God, we—and I don't care who it is— are doing something wrong. I had the same question in my mind when I was attacked with cancer, so I asked the Lord, "Why the attack on my body? You know I try to do everything right. I wouldn't deliberately do anything wrong for anything in this world. I don't allow any jealousy, envy, or strife in me. I want the best for everybody. So why the attack?" I recognized that I had to be doing something wrong when an attack like that happened, and I wanted to know why because if it could happen once, it could happen again.

During the whole time of my illness, people sent me all kind of stuff to try and help me—lots and lots of books and tapes; so many that I could fill a library room with all that was sent. I tried to read them, but there were just too many. But one book caught my attention. It had been sent by one of our TV viewers. What caught my eye was that it said, "You'll have lots of energy." I have always been busy, busy, busy. I always seemed, however, to have a low energy level. Most times I felt sluggish and might have even looked it, but I just kept going and pushing myself. This book, called *Fit for Life,* caught my attention. As I began to read it, I found out where I believed my problem was. It is not really a diet book, but it told me how to get my body in order, because my body was out of order and I didn't even realize it.

As a kid I had been brought up eating certain kinds of food. I came from a large family with twelve children, and the food we ate was not necessarily healthy. It was food to make one full, like: pork neck bones, rice, gravy, greens, red beans, macaroni and cheese, bread puddings. All of that good stuff. There wasn't a lot of nutrition in it, but it kept us alive. There are thousands and thousands of people, Christians included, who have all kinds of ailments caused by their bad nutritional habits.

Anyway, in reading this book, I found out I had a very toxic body. In the past, I had not eaten much fruit because we weren't brought up on fruit. We couldn't afford fruit. We got fruit for Christmas and that was it. I never ate a lot of raw salads and vegetables because we never had that. We did eat greens, but I found out later that all the nutrients were cooked out of them, so we were hardly getting any nutrients for our bodies. On top of that I loved coffee. I would drink coffee with my meals, before my meal, and after my meal. The authors of *Fit for Life* said that drinking coffee with your meals rushes the food into your intestines too fast, so the body doesn't get to do what it is supposed to do with digesting the food.[1] As a result, you become constipated. I had suffered from constipation almost all of my life. It ran in the family because we all ate the same thing. Eating the way the book recommended corrected that constipation. Again, you have to die to self, and you have to put the body under and do what you are supposed to do if you want the desired results.

I started eating fruit in the morning and salads and vegetables that were not overcooked for lunch and dinner. I didn't cut out all meats; the book doesn't tell you to do that. I told my kids about it, and they decided to try eating this way as well. Of course, this new approach to health was easy for Fred because when I fixed my meals I could do his as well. When I told Frederick about eating this way, I said, "You know, Frederick, one of the main writers of this book lived to be 109 eating like this." Freddie said, "No, I'm not eating that junk. I don't want to be 109." That's because he was only eleven years old. But this way of eating has worked well for both my husband and me.

We found out in raising our children that you want to have a pleasant environment for your children to come home to. You don't want to try and force your children to do something just because you like doing it, or try to make them come around to your point of view. Let them be who they are.

Like one family I'm thinking about now. The mother was just so hard on her kids. She would tell her children, "We're Christians now. You're not going to look at anything on television except Christian channels." They could not listen to music on the radio or play tapes. She made the children miserable. Where are the kids now? In the street—they don't believe God or anything. And mom is not making it either. You can go overboard living the "Christian life," more like a religious life. God doesn't call you to do that. He calls us to use wisdom. Listening to music is just a stage children go through. They'll eventually grow out of it. You have to make the environment nice for your children and don't put them in bondage, but let them see you doing right. Then they will know what to do at a given time.

If you disobey any laws, it causes a negative reaction to come upon your life, and that includes disobeying the dietary laws of good nutrition. I was disobeying dietary laws, and there was nothing God could do. No matter how much I was praying and making my confession that, "no evil shall befall me and no plague shall come near my dwelling" (Ps. 91:10), if I was doing something wrong to bring on that plague, it was going to come. You can name all the blessings you want from the Lord, but if you are doing certain things, like walking in the flesh—fornicating, lying, stealing, and doing all the other bad stuff—those blessings will not come. Just because God doesn't come down and strike someone dead when he or she is doing wrong doesn't mean that He approves of their actions. It is just that God is so merciful. But we can only depend upon His mercy for just so long. If we could just die to self and lay aside all of those things that would hinder us from moving in God and receiving His blessings, just think what the body of Christ could do in reaching the lost.

We certainly can't reach the lost if we are sick. A lot of Christians still smoke and drink excessively. And because God won't come down and take the cigarettes or alcohol from them, they keep on smoking and drinking, using the rationale, "Well, I'm going to die from something, so I may as well die from smoking." That is so stupid, because you don't realize what you are going to face when you get sick. Believe me; it is horrible to have to go through a sickness like I went through. When you deliberately sin, you are going to have to give an account to God. You may think you are getting away with something, but you are not.

The Bible tells us in Hebrews 12:1–2:

> Let us lay aside every weight, and the sin which so easily ensnares us, and let us run with endurance the race that is set before us, looking unto Jesus, the author and finisher of our faith.

You must decide for yourself that you will do anything you have to do to get in tune with Him. We are to "lay aside every weight, and the sin which so easily ensnares us." Jesus has provided everything we need to be winners in life.

> I beseech you therefore, brethren, by the mercies
> of God, that you present your bodies a living
> sacrifice, holy, acceptable to God, which is your
> reasonable service. And do not be conformed to
> this world, but be transformed by the renewing
> of your mind, that you may prove what is that
> good and acceptable and perfect will of God.
>
> —ROMANS 12:1–2

The reason many of us can't prove His good, perfect, and acceptable will for our lives is because we don't do what the Bible says to do. It is up to us to choose His way. He wants His peace and His blessings ruling in our lives. But it is up to us to choose what will rule in our lives—the blessings or the curses. As for me and my house, we want the blessings. What about you?

CHAPTER 4

WALKING IN HOLINESS

Let us cleanse ourselves from all filthiness.

—2 CORINTHIANS 7:1

HOLINESS MEANS TO BE SET apart for the service of God. If we were determined to serve God, a lot of things that are going on in the church today would not be going on. When we received Jesus Christ as Savior and Lord, we became born again, but some of us never grew from that point. We may go to church on Sunday, but we do what we want to do Monday through Saturday. We have not changed our souls. We keep gossiping, complaining, fornicating, lying, cheating— you name it. We keep doing all the same fleshly things we always did. Nobody would ever know we were born again by our actions. The sad thing is that when you are not living a holy life, you are cheating yourself, because you cut the blessings of God out of your life. God is not a part of anything that is not holy. Personally, I believe this is why so many Christians never get their prayers answered. They never receive the things they are most desirous of because they are not doing it God's way.

Holiness is a commandment of God. First Peter 1:15–16 tell us:

> As He who called you is holy, you also be holy in all your conduct, because it is written, "Be holy, for I am holy."

There are far too many Christians in churches and our workplaces who are falling short of this commandment. As the body of Christ, we are going to have to make up our minds that we want to be obedient to the Lord if we want His wonderful promises to work for us. One of the ways we can be obedient is to live holy. Some people have commented, "I don't really know how to be holy. How do you do that?" It's not hard. It is just a matter of being obedient to the Word of God. Obedience brings great rewards.

> I beseech you, therefore, brethren, by the mercies of God, that you present your bodies a living sacrifice, holy, acceptable to God, which is your reasonable service.
>
> —ROMANS 12:1

The way we begin to live holy is by presenting our bodies to God. Would you want God involved in all your circumstances? Can He go everywhere you go? Can He do everything you do? He sees everything you are doing anyway, so you need to think about that. It is simply a matter of being obedient to the Word.

Romans 12:2 says:

> And do not be conformed to this world, but be transformed by the renewing of your mind, that you may prove what is that good and acceptable and perfect will of God.

The only way you are going to be able to prove what is that "good, acceptable, and perfect will of God" is by renewing your mind.

You are born of the Word of God. You are born of water and of the Spirit. The water refers to the Word, so you need to feed yourself on the Word to grow spiritually. Believers don't realize that. They just think they can receive Jesus and believe in God, and that is all they need to do. Then they make their own rules about how they are going to live their lives, so they don't get the benefits that come from living a godly life. If you are not living the way you are supposed to be living as a Christian, I want to share with you some ways you can start getting yourself together so that you can enjoy life now, while you are here on this earth. The minute you become born again you are born into the kingdom of God, so you have covenant rights that include all the blessings of God talked about in the Bible. But these blessings don't just fall on you like rain. You have to grow up in the Word and you have to learn to work the Word in order to receive these blessings.

All throughout the New Testament in the Epistles (letters written to the early church by various writers), notice how often the Apostle Paul (who wrote most of these letters) talks about how we should live, what we should abstain from, what we should put on, and what we should put off. I know a lot of Christians don't read the Bible because I see in my own church too many people who walk opposite of what the Bible says. And I know my church is no different from anybody else's church. Far too many church members operate in their flesh rather than in the spirit. It was the same in Paul's time, and sad to say it is still the same way today.

> I speak in human terms because of the weakness of your flesh. For just as you presented your members as slaves of uncleanness, and of lawlessness leading to more lawlessness, so now present your members as slaves of righteousness for holiness.
> —ROMANS 6:19

It is our responsibility to do it. Just as we presented our members as slaves when we were in the world, Paul is telling us now that we are saved to present our members as righteousness for holiness in the Lord. We can do this. The Holy Spirit through the Apostle Paul would not tell us to do this if we couldn't do it. It says in Romans 6:22:

> But now having been set free from sin, and having become slaves of God, you have your fruit to holiness, and the end, everlasting life.

When we received Christ, we were set free from sin, but that does not mean we can't sin; we just don't have to. When Jesus died on the cross and shed His precious blood for us, which gave us the right to be set free from sin. So if you are sinning, you are doing it because you want to, not because you have to. When you were a sinner, you did not have any choice. But now you are born again and you have a new spirit. You have been set free from living that sinful life.

> But you have not so learned Christ, if indeed you have heard Him and have been taught by Him, as the truth is in Jesus [this is the way you live a holy life]: that you put off, concerning your former conduct, the old man which grows corrupt according to the deceitful lusts, and be renewed

in the spirit of your mind, and that you put on the
new man which was created according to God, in
true righteousness and holiness.

—EPHESIANS 4:20–24

It is up to us to put off the old man and to put on the
new man, and you put on the new man by spending
time in the Word of God and being obedient to what
the Word says. Now that old man will just pull on you
and try to keep you from living according to the new
man. But you are going to have to take control over that
old man and let your new man run your life. Otherwise,
you are going to be in trouble all your life—an up-and-
down Christian.

First Thessalonians 4:3–7:

> For this is the will of God, your sanctification:
> that you should abstain from sexual immorality;
> that each of you should know how to possess his
> own vessel in sanctification and honor [it is up to
> us to know how to control our own bodies], not
> in passion of lust, like the Gentiles who do not
> know God; that no one should take advantage of
> and defraud his brother in this matter, because
> the Lord is the avenger of all such, as we also
> forewarned you and testified. For God did not
> call us to uncleanness but in holiness.

God is calling us to live holy lives, and we are going to have to do the things that will cause us to live that life of holiness. Notice verse 6 says: "no one should take advantage of and defraud his brother in this matter." Anytime you get involved sexually with someone, and you are confessing to be a Christian, you are causing another person to sin and you are planting death in his or her life, as well as your own.

It is sad to say, but from the pulpit to the pew, Christian people are involved in adultery and fornication. They are killing themselves. They are certainly not walking in holiness, and God is not involved in their circumstances when they are involved in sin. I don't care what a good time you have at church shouting and singing every Sunday, if you are involved in that kind of thing, you are just moving by how you feel, and nothing really is happening in your life.

I read a book by a psychologist who was talking about the problems facing the women of today. I read the book trying to get some insight as to why there is so much strife, bitterness, envy, and jealousy in the church, especially among women. I am sorry to say this, but the psychologists don't have the answers either. One thing I did agree with the psychologist on was that a woman can live a fulfilled life without a man. This is what I have told women over and over:

"You belong to God. Build a relationship with Jesus Christ, who made you. He knows more about you than anybody. Be obedient to what He says, and He has the answer for you. He has the man for you." Philippians 4:19 explains that "my God shall supply all your need according to His riches in glory by Christ Jesus." That means more than finances. That means anything you need—a husband, if that is what you need. Trust your life to the Lord.

So many times we don't want to wait on God because the flesh is constantly pulling on us. But God has told us what to do about the flesh and that if we would do what He said to do, then He would bring into our lives that which would cause us to have the greatest fulfillment we could ever have. Can't you trust the Man who died for you? Wouldn't you think He wanted the very best for you? Build that relationship with the Lord, and then you will not have to go through so much heartache and heartbreak.

First Corinthians 3:16–17 tells us:

> Do you not know that you are the temple of God and that the Spirit of God dwells in you? If anyone defiles the temple of God, God will destroy him. For the temple of God is holy, which temple you are.

Think about God dwelling in you. Think about how, when you go to bed with someone who is not your husband, you are taking God to bed with you. All of this is in the Word, telling us how to live a holy life.

> Therefore, having these promises, beloved, let us [God is not going to do it] cleanse ourselves from all filthiness of the flesh and spirit, perfecting holiness in the fear of God.
>
> —2 CORINTHIANS 7:1

These are the ways we cleanse ourselves:

> Therefore laying aside all malice, all deceit, hypocrisy, envy, and all evil-speaking, as newborn babes, desire the pure milk of the word, that you may grow thereby.
>
> —1 PETER 2:1–2

Some Unholy Traits

I researched the definitions of these personality traits that Peter listed above, and I want to share them with you. These are the traits that cause so many problems in the body of Christ, which we need to get rid of if we are going to walk in holiness.

Malice

Malice means two things: In a general sense, it means wickedness and all forms of evil. It is a word that covers all the vices of man. In Romans 1:29–32, we see some of these vices. This is really talking about the world, but we see some Christians acting the same way also:

> Being filled with all unrighteousness, sexual immorality, wickedness, covetousness, maliciousness; full of envy, murder strife, deceit, evil-mindedness; they are whisperers, backbiters, haters of God, violent, proud, boasters, inventors of evil things, disobedient to parents, undiscerning, untrustworthy, unloving, unforgiving, unmerciful; who, knowing the righteous judgment of God, that those who practice such things are deserving of death, not only do the same but also approve of those who practice them.

Some Christians who attend church regularly do these kinds of things. They shouldn't do them, and God does not approve of what they are doing.

The second definition of *malice,* in a narrow sense, means harboring deep-seated resentment against a person or having a hatred for someone that goes on and on. I know Christians like this who had a long-lasting bitterness against a person. It means ill will, actually wishing that something bad would happen to a person. Isn't that terrible for a Christian to feel like that against another Christian? But sadly, it happens.

Deceit

Deceit means to deceive and mislead people; to deceive in order to achieve one's own end. It also means to be two-faced. Guile and deception have to do primarily with words. For example, when a person wants something from another person, he or she tries to get it by using flattery: "Oh, you sure look nice." But in the back of her mind, she's thinking, "She looks awful." Just because she wants to get something from that person, she will use insincere flattery. There are some strong-willed people in the church who entice weak people to follow them. They use people for their own gain. They operate in deceit, being covetous. You need to know the Word, so that when these type of people come around you, you will know how to deal with them.

Hypocrisy

Hypocrisy means pretending to be something or someone you are not. The reason why Peter and the other writers of the New Testament wrote the Epistles to the early church was because the same things that are going on today in churches were going on back then. It really is sad that we still have to deal with the same problems among Christians. You see a lot of hypocrisy among people in the church who are seeking a position of leadership and authority, and it should not be that way. Hypocrisy is one of the traits God hates the most.

Envy

Envy means to covet what someone else has. People envy other people's money, position, looks, possessions, popularity, and authority. It is hard for me to understand why anyone would be envious or jealous of anybody, because it doesn't help in any way to be envious and really only hurts the person doing the envying. And after you have gone through all the frustration of being jealous and envious, the people you are envious of still have whatever you were envying them for. So you go through all that stuff for nothing. Why can't we grow up and learn that God is no respecter of persons? What He will do for one, He will do for another. So just believe God for what you want instead of envying someone because of what they have.

There was a woman in the church who used to sew for me. She was an excellent seamstress. She also dressed very nicely because she made a lot of her own clothes.

When she started sewing for me, some of the members started talking negatively about her. That is so dumb. They talked about not only her, but anybody who does things for me, Fred, and our children. We have to have some things done for us. Because we stay so much on the go, we ask the people who service us to come to our home. They do our nails, hair, and what have you. When some of the members found out about it, they started talking about the people who were providing us these services out of jealousy. Why? We are not God.

We as Christians still have much to learn about doing what God wants us to do so that we can walk in holiness and be more like Jesus, instead of looking at our brothers and sisters ready to criticize. Envy takes a terrible toll on the body and on the emotions. That is why Proverbs 14:30 says:

> A sound heart is life to the body. But envy is rottenness to the bones.

You want to have a good, healthy heart and a pure heart. If you want to have rottenness in your bones, keep operating in envy; it will catch up with you in the long run.

Evil-speaking

Evil-speaking means to criticize, judge, backbite, gossip, condemn, censor, and grumble against another person. There is far too much of that in the body of Christ. Too many Christians love to hear bad news about somebody. It doesn't even have to be true, but we just love to hear it. We love to talk about people's downfalls. It is terrible for us as Christians to have this kind of attitude. Whenever you do that, you are planting seeds of corruption for yourself. You are going to have the downfall. I would never even rejoice at my enemy's downfall. What I would want my enemy to do is to repent and come out of his situation. But I would not want him to suffer.

We need to get control of gossip. There is too much of it tearing up the church. God doesn't like it. We are supposed to be examples of Jesus Christ. People come to church to get help, and pastors can't help the people from the outside who need help because of the need to help the people on the inside. We should be examples. When people see us, they should see Jesus. They should say, "I want what you have." But if we are gossiping and talking about everybody in or out of the church, we will turn the people away. Do you realize that you can say something negative and turn people off from coming to church for life, and they can end up in hell? I wouldn't want that on my conscience.

First Peter 2:9 tells us:

> But you are a chosen generation, a royal priesthood, a holy nation, His own special people, that you may proclaim the praises of Him who called you out of darkness into His marvelous light.

You need to know you are royalty, His own special people. The word *peculiar* means "special." It does not mean we are supposed to look funny, like some denominations teach: "Don't wear makeup; no jewelry, no pants." No, it means we are God's special people, and we need to live like that.

> Who once were not a people but are now the people of God, who had not obtained mercy, but now have obtained mercy. [How grateful we should be for God's mercy. That is why we should want to live as much like God as we possibly can.] Beloved, I beg you [I urge you, I exhort you] as sojourners and pilgrims, abstain from fleshly lusts which war against the soul, having your conduct honorable among the Gentiles, that when they speak against you as evildoers, they may, by your good works which they observe, glorify God in the day of visitation.
>
> —1 PETER 2:10–12

Yes, we might be talked about, but don't let it be true what they are saying. Christians are going to be talked about—the Bible says so. The devil hates us for being Christians. We just don't want God talking about us.

Teaching Our Children to Live Holy Lives

You need to shoot for the very best for your children. Yes, they are in the world, and they have feelings because they are just like other children. You need to talk very openly with your children. That is what Fred and I did; therefore, we were able to raise our children without any serious problems. I told my children— daughters and son—no sex before marriage. They were taught that from their early teen years when they began to notice the opposite sex. I knew they could abstain because I did it. I made up my mind when I was a teenager that I was not going to be involved with anybody sexually until I got married. It is just a matter of making that choice. I encouraged our children never to put themselves in the position of doing the wrong thing, saying the wrong thing, or touching the wrong places. And I encourage you to tell your children the same thing. I know that a lot of psychologists, coun- selors, and teachers say that having sex after a certain age is normal, but that is not what the Bible says.

As I said, Fred and I discussed everything with our children because we knew what they had facing them as Christians in a world where anything goes. We told them there was nothing wrong with sex and that God made it to be enjoyed. But there is a time for sex, and it is in marriage. I do not believe in kids going steady, where they go off by themselves with their dates. That invites trouble. But we did want our kids to enjoy life, so when our son was a teenager and he wanted to take a girl out on a date, my husband or myself would double date with him or his sisters and their husbands would go out with them. Of course, as he matured and made plans to be married, it was a different story. Some parents may say, "Well, the teenagers don't like being chaperoned. How did you get your son to do that?" Well, I am the one who carried him nine months and went through all that trouble to bring him into the world when I was at an older age, so I am the one who is making the rules in my house. If he didn't want to go out with any of us on a double date, he did not go out. When Freddie met his wife Angel and they seriously talked of marriage, naturally they went out alone. But more often, he and Angel went out with their friends in a group or with his sisters and their husbands. Some people say, "Well, kids have a way to do stuff if they want to." I would warn Frederick when he was looking at girls, "If you like a girl and this girl puts you in a compromised position or you her, I'm going to know it, because I'm open to God and I believe He will let me know what is going on with my children." Make rules for your children, then you put them in God's hands. You are going to have to make decisions for your children because they are your responsibility until they are old enough to be on their own.

You have to let them know that they cannot trust their flesh. You cannot turn your back on it. The flesh is strong and difficult to control, and it never lets up its assaults against the will. I know, because I have a challenge with eating. I love to eat, and if I have to watch myself or I would have a problem with my weight. I would say, "I am not going to eat that stuff." Then, before I knew it, I had eaten it. And I paid the price for it, too. The flesh is forever pulling at you. You have to say, "No. No." That is what you do with anything regarding the flesh.

The Works of the Flesh that
Prevent a Life of Holiness

Galatians 5:19–21 tells us:

> Now the works of the flesh are evident, which
> are: adultery, fornication, uncleanness, lewdness,

idolatry, sorcery, hatred, contentions, jealousies, outbursts of wrath, selfish ambitions, dissensions, heresies, envy, murders, drunkenness, revelries, and the like; of which I tell you beforehand, just as I also told you in time past, that those who practice such things will not inherit the kingdom of God.

Now where it says, "Those who practice such things will not inherit the kingdom of God," it does not mean that these people are not saved. It simply means that they will not enjoy the blessings that Jesus came to give, which are prosperity, peace, joy, and freedom from sin. Because God is not involved in your life when you are in sin. I did some research on some of these hindrances to living a holy life, and I found these meanings:

Adultery is sexual unfaithfulness to a husband or wife. There are too many Christians who are unfaithful to their husbands or wives, even in the church. I talk to people who are challenged with this problem all the time. When you commit adultery, you are operating in the flesh and cutting God out of your life.

Fornication is a broad word that includes all forms of immoral and sexual acts, such as pre-marital sex, homosexuality, lesbianism, and any form of abnormal sexual activity. Sadly, there is far too much fornication among Christians, and it hurts the body of Christ badly.

Uncleanness or lewdness means moral impurity, doing things that are dirty, polluted, and disgusting.

Lasciviousness means "filthiness," "indecency," and "shamefulness."

Idolatry is the worship of idols, whether spiritual or material. It is the worship of some idea of what God is like, of an image of God within a person's mind. It involves the giving of one's primary devotion, time, and energy to something other than God. Idolatry could be the worship of anything or anyone: your husband, children, house, car, profession—anything. We need to be careful to what and where we give our time and energy.

Sorcery refers to the practice of witchcraft, the use of drugs, or the involvement with evil spirits in order to gain control over the lives of others. It includes all forms of seeking to control one's fate, including astrology, palm reading, séances, fortune telling, crystals, and other forms of witchcraft. If you are engaged in anything like that, it is not of God and you need to stop it.

The evil thing that stands out the most to me is an individual taking control of someone else's life. There are people who can't go anywhere without a particular person being with them or they cannot do anything unless that person is there. We should not allow a person to control us. There are Christian leaders who take advantage of people because the people are weak and are easily led. You have to watch these types of people who want to control others.

Hatred means "enmity," "hostility," and "animosity." This type of hatred lingers on and on, deep within. If you have feelings like that, you really need to seek the Lord to help you get rid of that hatred, because it can do you harm.

Variance is strife, discord, contentions, fighting, quarreling, dissension, and wrangling. It means to fight against another person in order to get something, such as a position, promotion, honor, or recognition. It happens when people deceive and are willing to do whatever it takes to get what he or she is after. We sure have experienced that in our church, and I am sure other churches have the same challenge with people. The pastor cannot control it, even though he is the leader. The pastor cannot be responsible for what everybody is doing in the church. There are people who form cliques with this group or that group. They cause division in the church, one clique fighting for position against another, doing little mean things to keep people from being in a certain position in the church. All for recognition and honor.

That kind of honor is not worth it. I would not want a position if I would have to hurt somebody else to get it, but people do that in our church. When we become aware of it, we try to do something about it. It is sad that people form cliques in the church, and they need to be broken up wherever they are. Cliques should not be in the body of Christ. We are all one in Christ or at least should be.

Emulations means "wanting and desiring to have what someone else has." It may be material things, recognition, honor, or position. And that, too, is found in the church.

Wrath refers to indignation, a violent explosive temper, and anger. Quick and explosive reactions that arise from violent emotions. It is anger that fades away just as quickly as it arose, not anger that lasts. That is the difference between wrath and hatred. Hatred lasts on and on, while wrath is quick and explosive.

Strife is conflict, struggle, fighting, contentions, factions, and dissensions. People get into strife quickly because a lot of times they want to have authority over others. Oftentimes, in large churches they will make up their own little kingdom so they can be the king and queen over everybody in their group. If God has called you to a place, He is no respecter of persons; let Him put you in that place. Don't fight and complain about not getting a certain position and cause division in the church, because you will help drive people away. How can we draw unsaved people to Christ if we are fussing, fighting, and in strife with one another? Church, we are going to have to work on that. I know it is not just my church, but all churches have problems with people being cliquish and causing strife. Naturally, we know that the devil is the instigator. He is going to come in and fight against the body from within to try to keep it from moving in the peace, joy, and unity that represent Jesus Christ, but we have overcome him with God's Word.

Seditions means divisions, rebellion, standing against others, and splitting off from others. Too much of that is going on in the church.

Heresies involves rejecting the fundamental beliefs of God, Christ, the Scriptures, and the church. It means believing and holding to some teaching other than the truth of the Word.

Murder means to kill or to take the life of another person. But you can also murder with your tongue by gossiping about someone, killing somebody's character, and killing somebody's relationship with another person. We really need to avoid gossiping and talking about people, especially a brother or sister in the church.

Drunkenness means taking drink or drugs to affect one's senses for lust or pleasure, becoming tipsy or intoxicated, or seeking bodily or sexual pleasure through drink or drugs. It goes without saying that Christians should not be involved in anything like drunkenness or drugs.

Revellings means "carousing," "uncontrolled indulgence," and "pleasure." Taking part in wild parties and drinking parties and indulging in feeding the lusts of the flesh is characteristic of revellings.

It is a fact that the flesh wars against the spirit, but if we want to walk in holiness, we have to control our urges, desires, and passions. We have to do like Hebrews 12:14 says: "Pursue peace with all people, and holiness, without which no one will see the Lord." To pursue peace means to follow after peace. So if you are following after peace, you are not operating in any of those things I listed above that cause divisions, strife, and the other evil things that will stop you from walking in holiness.

CHAPTER 5

A SOUND HEART

A sound heart is life of the body.
—PROVERBS 14:30

THE WORD *SOUND* MEANS "MEDICINE, curative, calm." That type of heart or spirit is the life of the flesh. If you want your flesh to have a good life or to have the very best God has for you, then you need a sound heart or a developed spirit. In other words, you are growing in God's Word and developing your spirit man. The second part of Proverbs 14:30 says, "but envy is rottenness to the bones."

There is just too much envy, jealousy, and strife in the body of Christ. I believe this is why there are a lot of negative things and sicknesses taking place among Christians. God has given us directions to follow His Word to have a good life, but somehow we want to skirt the Word and go down to the level of our flesh and its experiences.

Some Christian friends of mine, a husband and wife, attended a church where they were dealing with homosexual pastors and leaders. (There really should not be a question concerning homosexuals in leadership in the church because God specifically deals with the problem of homosexuality in the book of Romans. All this church needed to do was follow the Bible.) This couple considers themselves to be very logical and sound people, as well as good Christians. They indicated, in so many words, that they believed homosexuality was the way people were born and that they did not have a choice in the matter. One of them had had an experience in their home where a person was a homosexual, and the couple could not understand why this person had turned out to be that way. The guy said, "This person came up in the same home that I did and was raised the same way I was. Why did he turn out like that?" I told them I really did not know, and I don't believe anyone really knows, except the Lord. But God's Word tells us that people are not born this way. It is a choice they make.

My friend said, "Well, you know there are university professors, doctors, and teachers who are coming out of the closet, telling the world they are homosexuals and lesbians." I said to them, "These people consider themselves to be very intelligent and intellectual. But spiritually they are not, because if they were, they would follow God's Word." In order to get the very best out of life, I believe people should get all the academic learning possible, but academic learning is not above God's Word. The Bible says that "all the treasures of wisdom and knowledge" are hidden in Christ Jesus (Col. 2:3), so we can look to God's Word when it comes right down to dealing with human problems. Of course, I know that the problems of homosexuality and lesbianism are very real to many people, but that is not the way God told us to walk. If you find yourself in that kind of situation, a choice has to be made as to which way you want to go: are you going to follow what the Word says, or are you going the way of the world? The world says, anything goes. But that is not what the Bible says. If you want to receive God's best, you have to have a sound heart, which will produce a sound mind.

When this couple asked me what I thought about homosexuality, all I did was go to the Word of God. These logical Christians were trying to say that perhaps God did not mean what was said in the Bible. I told them that Romans 1:28 said that the people did not like to retain God in their knowledge, so He gave them over to a debased (or a reprobate) mind. The word "reprobate" means "a mind void of judgment." I said to them, "You can see that homosexuality or lesbianism is caused by a mind void of judgment. I don't care how smart or intellectual they are, their minds are void of judgment. Two men cannot have a baby, and two women cannot have a baby. They can adopt all the kids they want, but it is not a real family in the sense that God meant a family to be." The guy said, "Well, I'm not concerned about that. I don't want to be the judge of these people." God has told us to judge sin when we see it (not the sinner—that is His job). I am concerned about the fact that these homosexual couples will take children into their homes where they will act as the children's parents or guardians. What can they teach these kids? How can they say that two men or two women living together is the description of parenting God had in mind when He told Adam and Eve in Genesis 1:28: "Be fruitful and multiply; fill the earth"?

This is something we, as Christians, have to deal with. We cannot try to make an excuse for people living in sin, even if we don't want to call it sin. My friend said, "Well, maybe God knew not everybody was going to be homosexual. He knew that He would have enough people who would be heterosexual that the race would carry on, and then He would have another group of people who would live their lives as homosexuals." I could not believe that rational Christians would be making these kinds of observations instead of believing what God plainly says in the Bible. It is sad to say, but obviously they do not have sound hearts.

What Is in Your Heart?

The heart (figuratively speaking) stands for man's mental and moral activity, including both the rational and emotional elements. Obviously, this is not talking about the part of man's anatomy that pumps blood throughout his body. Some biblical teachers teach that the *heart* is actually the human spirit. There are many references to the heart, the soul, and the spirit. Sometimes the word *heart* is referring to the soul and sometimes to the spirit. When people read the Bible, they need to rely on the Holy Spirit to interpret when it is referring to the heart or the spirit. The Bible describes human depravity as being in the heart, because sin has its seat in the center of man's inward life—the heart or the spirit.

When you received Jesus Christ, you received Him into your heart. The Scriptures regard the heart as the sphere of divine influence. (See Romans 10:8–9.) We really do not know all that is in people's hearts because you cannot see the heart. But when you hear people talk, you can usually tell what is in their hearts. You can talk to Christians, and you know right away that they have not crucified that old man that is in their hearts. The old man and the new man are both in the heart together—the old man with all the ugliness and the evil, and the new man with a Christ-like nature. When you become born again, you have to take that new man through God's Word and get rid of all that negative and ugly stuff that has been in the old man; that is, if you choose to. Otherwise, you can hold on to the old man. A lot of Christians hold on to him. They are born again, but that is all. The body of Christ could be a lot further along if we all chose to live according to the new man.

God gives us laws to follow, and He expects us to obey them. We can obey them because we have a free will. After you become born again, you should be able to obey God's laws because you are a brand new person in Christ. If you give yourself to the Word, that will help you to obey God and drive out all the negative stuff that is in your heart. The heart includes the emotions, the reason, and the will.[1] When we live in disobedience, we keep getting further and further down into the hardness of the heart, where even God cannot reach you. I believe that this is what happens with those who choose to live in homosexuality. We are now in the last days when wickedness and lawlessness are coming out more than ever before. There are even some people who want to believe that homosexuality is just like being born in a minority race. That is just plain ridiculous. People do not make a choice as to what color or race they are going to be when they come into the world. But homosexuals can choose to be what they are.

Proverbs 4:20–22 tells us:

> My son, give attention to my words; Incline your ear to my sayings. Do not let them depart from your eyes; Keep them in the midst of your heart; For they are life to those who find them, And health to all their flesh.

If you want good health and a blessed life, do not let God's Word depart from your eyes. If God's Word were constantly before our eyes, we would not engage in a lot of the sin and the negative stuff that have become a part of our daily living.

> Keep your heart with all diligence, for out of it spring the issues of life.
>
> —Proverbs 4:23

The issues of life come from the heart. I believe the reasons we see so much negative activity in the lives of Christians is because they don't deal with the things that are in their hearts. If they would replace the negative things with God's Word, they could drive those negative things out of their lives.

> My son, do not forget my law, but let your heart keep my commands; For length of days and long life And peace they will add to you. Let not mercy and truth forsake you; Bind them around your neck, Write them on the tablet of your heart. And so find favor and high esteem In the sight of God and man.
>
> —Proverbs 3:1–4

Isn't that beautiful. It is so simple. All we have to do is to obey. This is our responsibility as Christians. Do you want favor with God and man? Then don't let God's Word depart from your eyes. Keep His commandments. It doesn't matter what is going on around you. If you have favor with God, you will have favor with man.

> Trust in the Lord with all your heart, And lean not on your own understanding; In all your ways acknowledge Him, And He shall direct your paths. Do not be wise in your own eyes; fear the Lord and depart from evil. It will be health to your flesh, And strength to your bones.
>
> —Proverbs 3:5–8

Learn how to keep healthy by using God's Word.

I am sure as you read the following scriptures, you

can think of a lot of Christians who act in some of these negative ways:

> These six things the Lord hates, Yes, seven are an abomination to Him: A proud look, A lying tongue, Hands that shed innocent blood, A heart that devises wicked plans, Feet that are swift in running to evil, A false witness who speaks lies, And one who sows discord among brethren.
> —Proverbs 6:16–19

I know you are familiar with those kinds of activities with Christians. You would not even know they have the new man in the heart. "A proud look, a lying tongue"— there are too many Christians who lie without thinking. You know why they do it? Because lying is in their hearts and they have not dealt with it. Some Christians lie all the time. They look at you right in the face and lie, and you know they are lying. They know they are lying, but they have lied so much they have gotten hard hearts, and don't even realize they are lying.

The Heart and Mouth Work Together

Proverbs 16:23 says:

> The heart of the wise teaches his mouth, And adds learning to his lips.

In studying the heart and its actions, I found out that the mouth and the heart work together, because what is in the heart in abundance is going to come out of the mouth.

We have to understand that not every idea that comes to our minds come from our own minds. We are not always the ones who come up with something negative. There are evil spirits that can speak to our mind and influence our thinking. You should know that and beware. You have to be strong enough on the inside (in the spirit man) to know that when something negative comes to your mind that is against God's Word, it is not always you thinking it up. Don't ever act on a thought that is contrary to the Word. If you don't act on it and don't speak it out, it can never affect you.

He who has a deceitful heart finds no good, And he who has a perverse tongue falls into evil. [Look at that—*heart and tongue.*]
—PROVERBS 17:20

A merry heart does good, like medicine, but a broken spirit dries the bones.
—PROVERBS 17:22

It is up to us to keep our hearts merry, and the way to do that is to program your heart with God's Word. We cannot get away from God's Word. That is how I got through those horrible two years when I was believing God for my healing. I would encourage myself. There were times I felt like getting down in the dumps, just like everybody else. But we do not walk by feelings. We walk by faith.

> Bless the Lord, O my soul, And forget not all His benefits; Who forgives all your iniquities, Who heals all your diseases, Who redeems your life from destruction, Who crowns you with loving-kindness and tender mercies, Who satisfies your mouth with good things.
>
> —PSALM 103:2–5

When you want to encourage yourself in the Word, you tell yourself all the good things from God's Word and know that God is not a liar. The Bible says that He redeems our lives from destruction and crowns us with lovingkindness and tender mercies.

You have to keep your eyes on the Word and build yourself up on the Word when your countenance is low and you are going through something. God's Word is life. It is Spirit and it is life, and it will bring you life when you feel down.

> Blessed are the pure in heart, For they shall see
> God.
>
> —MATTHEW 5:8

You want to see God? Keep your heart pure. It is up to you to keep your heart pure, even though you may not do everything right. If you have confessed Jesus Christ as your personal Lord and Savior, you will go to heaven when you die. But if you obey the Word now, you can experience the kingdom of God here on earth. God will be manifested in and through your life through the Word. You don't have to wait until you die to experience the kingdom.

The Word Sown in the Heart

In Mark 4:14–20, Jesus talks about the sower sowing the Word. We know the ground is the heart:

> The sower sows the word. And these are the ones by the wayside where the word is sown. When they hear, Satan comes immediately and takes away the word that was sown in their hearts. These likewise are the ones sown on stony ground who, when they hear the word, immediately receive it with gladness; and they have no root in themselves, and so endure only for a time. Afterward,

when tribulation or persecution arises for the word's sake, immediately they stumble.

—MARK 4:14–17

Pastors and pastors' wives can relate to this scripture. Obviously, the Word is sown on stony ground when, at the least little thing, some people are gone. They endure for a season, and they seem to receive the Word gladly because it sounds good. They don't understand that when it comes to fighting that good fight of faith, there is a stand against the enemy that has to take place. Satan doesn't want us to enter into God's best, so he comes to steal the Word.

Now these are the ones sown among thorns; they are the ones who hear the word, and the cares of this world, the deceitfulness of riches, and the desires for other things entering in choke the word, and it becomes unfruitful.

—MARK 4:18–19

I can think of hundreds of instances where this has happened to people. Thousands come to the church and receive the Word of God, but the cares of this life and the deceitfulness of riches come in. They allow the Word to be stolen from them because they don't continue in it. Jesus says in John 8:31–32, "If you abide in My word, you are My disciples indeed. And you shall know the truth, and the truth shall make you free." You can't just hear the Word and be happy about it one time. You have to continue in it. And the Bible says if you continue in it, the Word will make you free—and that is free from anything that holds you in bondage.

> But these are the ones sown on good ground, those who hear the word, accept it, and bear fruit: some thirtyfold, some sixty, and some a hundred.
>
> —MARK 4:20

Thank God, He always has a remnant of people who will be fruitful and faithfully serve Him. These are the ones who carry on the work of the ministry. Thank God for people like that.

God wants us all to prosper. He wants us all to be fruitful and to be an example to the world that Jesus is Lord. Third John 2 says:

> Beloved, I pray that you may prosper in all things and be in health, just as your soul prospers.

You have to get this scripture into your heart by making it a part of your daily confessions: Your prayer could be something like this: "Father, I thank you that I am prospering in all things that you have made available to me in your Word. I am prospering in spirit, soul, body, and finances because of what Jesus did to set me free."

You have to confess God's Word before you see it take place in your life. You have to confess, "I believe all my needs are met," before you see all your needs met. That is your faith talking. But you have to be sure you believe it and are not just saying it without meaning. If you don't believe it, what you are confessing will not come to pass. But if you believe it and confess it, I am a living witness that it will come to pass.

Fred and I came from nothing financially. However, once we were exposed to God's Word, we started working the principles of faith, and we watched God start manifesting things in our lives. Not only material things, but even our spiritual growth jumped ahead. We believed that we received, and then we acted in concert with what we were confessing and believing. If you don't believe that you receive and you start crying, whining, and saying you are not going to make it, you will not get what God has promised in His Word. Don't try to figure out how He is going to bring it to you. That is not up to you. That is up to Him. Your part is to confess and believe you receive.

The way you know if you are believing something in your heart is that you will have a peace about you. You are not out there trying to beg, borrow, and steal from everybody. If you are believing in your heart, you don't have to ask anybody. God will lay it upon different people's hearts to give to you. I am a giver, but I don't like people to beg from me. I believe God will lead me to the ones who really need. No one likes a moocher, but there are some Christians who are always mooching off their brothers and sisters in the Lord. The Bible says in 2 Thessalonians 3:10, "If anyone will not work, neither shall he eat." If you are mooching because you don't want to work, that is not right. But if you are doing all that you know to do and your needs still are not met, that is a different story. You need to find out what you are doing wrong and correct it. God has a way of multiplying and giving you the abundance you need in your life, but you have to believe it in your heart.

I remember when we needed a new location to build a bigger church. The church on Crenshaw Boulevard in Inglewood had gotten too small for all the people who were coming there on Sundays. We had been out of room for years, so we, as a congregation, began to believe God to help us find a bigger place to hold our services. We really didn't know which way to go, but we never let our faith waiver because Fred always said, "It is God's problem. He is sending us the people, so it is up to Him to provide us a place." Therefore, we held fast to our confession of faith. We did not know how we were going to take care of the congregation and have enough room for them to be comfortable, but someone came and told us (while we were standing in faith) that Pepperdine University's campus was up for sale. It had been for sale for two years and we didn't even know about it.

God had it for us all the time; He was just waiting for somebody to dare to believe Him. God will walk over ten thousand people to honor a person who is believing Him. People had been trying to buy this property without success. Even the City of Los Angeles tried to buy it and they could not do it. Why? Because God was saving it for us. You don't have to try to figure out how God is going to bring something to pass. You just be right in your heart with the Lord. Let people say all the negative things they want to say about you; just know that it is the devil trying to get you down to keep you from having faith in God. Let the people talk, as long as what they are saying is not true. If it is not true, it cannot hurt you. If people only realized the damage they do to themselves by their negative conversations, they would not allow those words to come out of their mouths. When we hear about the negative things people say about us and our children, I just say, "Father, forgive them for they know not what they do." Then I tell the Lord to send forth laborers to minister to them to help them because they are hurting themselves and don't even know it. You don't have to fight back. You just make sure your heart is right and clean, and God will be on your side.

> We are more than conquerors through Him who loved us.
>
> —ROMANS 8:37

If you don't know how to activate the Word in your life, you can quote this scripture all you want to, but it will not have any affect on your life. You will not experience being more than a conqueror. I know because before I learned about faith, I would quote this scripture all the time, but I was not a conqueror. I was defeated and scared of everything: afraid of the dark, afraid to stay at home at night by myself, just fearful all the time. Once we learned about the principles of faith, I would say to myself, "I can't confess that I'm scared, so I'm going to have to get this out of my system." Then in the midst of that, when we first got involved in the Charismatic movement, people would bring us all kinds of tapes by different speakers to listen to. Someone gave me a tape about demons, and after I listened to it, I was even more petrified. The man who was speaking on the tape said that everybody had a demon. He said that he went into his bathroom and "coughed up a demon." That tape made me more afraid than ever. In addition to all the other fears I had, now I had "demons" to worry about.

When we first started trying to understand faith, there were some of us who would get together to listen to various faith teachers on tape. We would meet in a room at the church, or sometimes we would go to a friend's home to listen to these tapes. One night we were in the room at the church and someone sent this tape on demons. This was all very new to us, but we wanted to know more about faith and the Holy Spirit, so we listened to everything we could get our hands on. After hearing the speaker say that everyone had a demon, the people's minds started playing tricks on them. A lady sitting next to me said, "I have 19 demons." Another lady across from her said, "I have 38 demons." I could not move. I thought, "I'm scared of dogs and of people breaking into the house, but at least I can get away from a dog. If someone breaks in, I can run and hide somewhere. But demons are everywhere, and you can't even see them." I was so scared that I didn't leave that room until the next morning. We stayed there all night talking and praying.

The next day I found scriptures on fear, and I learned them all in one afternoon. My favorite one was 2 Timothy 1:7: "For God has not given us a spirit

of fear, but of power and of love and of a sound mind."
(It is still one of my favorites today.) I also learned the
Ninety-first Psalm. I began to confess: "He shall give
His angels charge of me." I also learned what it says in
Ephesians 6. I learned that we wrestle not against flesh
and blood but against spirits, and we have authority
over these spirits. You will not know about your
authority, if you have not been taught about who you
are in Christ.

> You are of God, little children [talking about
> Christians], and have overcome them, because
> He [Jesus] who is in you is greater than he [Satan]
> who is in the world.
>
> —1 JOHN 4:4

It didn't happen overnight, but as I began to confess
these scriptures, I finally got the victory over the fears
that had troubled me most all of my life. I fought
those fears for six months. I would lie in bed with my
husband right there beside me and would be as scared
as I could be of the demons because I believed they
were watching me, even though I could not see them.
Sometimes I could not sleep all night thinking of the
demons in the room. I had to confess those scriptures
over and over again until I drove fear out of my life.

That is what you have to do with anything you are

believing God for. You can't go by what you feel. Yes, there were times I felt afraid, but I did not confess what I felt. I confessed what I believed. I confessed that I didn't have the spirit of fear, but of power, love, and a sound mind. The same thing works in the opposite: you make a negative confession, and you are going to have a negative reaction. If you have a challenge with any of those sins of the flesh—adultery, fornication, murders, thefts, envy, strife, jealousy—you have to confess and believe you are free from them, and then start acting like you are free and don't commit that sin again. You don't have to confess it to anyone else; it is between you and God, but you say it loud enough so you can hear it.

You confess when you are ready to do something wrong, such as adultery or fornication. Before you commit these sins, you confess, "I'm going to meet you over there." Those words are coming out of your mouth. So why not change those words and say, "I'm free from that. I don't do that kind of thing (fornicate) any more, and so I will not be meeting you there (the motel). How about giving me a ring first? How about setting a wedding date first? I'll meet you at the altar."

If you believe you are healed, you have to confess that you believe you are healed and then thank God every day for your healing. Your confession every day should be: "I believe I'm healed based on God's Word:

that Jesus Himself took my infirmities and bore my sicknesses on the cross, and with His stripes, I am healed." (See Matthew 8:17 and I Peter 2:24.) Confess these scriptures instead of how you feel, and then do the things you are supposed to do. If you are under a doctor's care, continue to see your doctor. We never said not to go to the doctor. People have lied and said Fred told them not to consult doctors. That is not true. If you will go back to the very first book Fred wrote in 1976, *How Faith Works,* he explains that medicine has nothing to do with your faith, unless you put your faith in the medicine or the doctor. Actually, you may need the medicine and the care of the doctor while you are standing on the Word in faith.

Determine to be so full of the Word and the Spirit of God that what is in you is stronger than anything around you, and God will see you through anything you have to face and will give you the life of victory that is rightfully yours as a believer in Jesus Christ. He is not a respecter of persons. What He says to me, He says to you. We can all be winners if we will get all of the junk out of our hearts and minds. Then we will be the body of Christ the world is so very desperately in need of. We have the answers the world needs. That is why we have to make sure our hearts are pure and sound if we want to affect the world for Jesus and bring the lost into the kingdom.

CHAPTER 6

A PROSPEROUS SOUL

That you may prosper in all things...just as
your soul prospers.

—3 JOHN 2

THIRD JOHN 2 SAYS THAT if your soul is not prospering, the rest of you will not be prospering either. Our souls are not saved yet, and neither are our bodies. Only our spirits are saved when we become born again. I believe that all the problems in the body of Christ begin in the area of the soul. Sometimes people get the soul and the spirit mixed up. They think they are operating in the spirit, when really they are operating in the soul.

The soul contains your will, emotions, intellect, and desires. It is what makes up your personality—which is the thing that makes us different from one another. We have to possess or take control of our souls, because if we don't we will never reach the high calling of God.

Man is a three-part (tripartite) creature, made up of spirit, soul, and body. The spirit should be governed by the Holy Spirit and the Word of God. As believers in the Lord Jesus Christ, that means we have to get our souls—which contain our minds—renewed by the Word of God. Then the soul and body can be governed by our recreated spirit. So many Christians are ruled by the soulish area of their being because most of the time they don't even hear the Word taught. They go to churches where they may hear an energetic message that may move them emotionally, but they are not taught the Word. Consequently, they can only live by what they think or how they feel.

To put it in a nutshell, the spirit man is that part of the believer that is like God. The soulish man is dominated by his mind and free will, and he is always looking to please the self. The carnal man is ruled by fleshly desires. At the new birth, we receive a new spirit man. In 2 Corinthians, 5:17 it says, "If anyone is in Christ, he is a new creation; old things have passed away; behold, all things have become new." Only the spirit is new. The soul and body are the same as they were before the re-birth of the spirit man. It is up to the recreated spirit man to do something about the soulish man and carnal man.

The Apostle Paul tells us in Romans 12:1–2 that we can "prove what is that good, acceptable and perfect will of God" for our lives if we would renew our minds with God's Word:

> I beseech you therefore, brethren, by the mercies of God, that you present your bodies a living sacrifice, holy, acceptable to God, which is your reasonable service. And do not be conformed to this world, but be transformed by the renewing of your mind, that you may prove what is that good and acceptable and perfect will of God.

It is the Bible that tells us how we are to live and instructs us not to go by what the world says. I know a lot of Christians have not renewed their minds because a lot of things they do is coming from the soulish area and not the spirit. If they had renewed their minds, they would do what the Word says. The Bible says we are to love one another. Therefore, if you loved your brothers and sisters, you would not talk about them, gossip about them, or tell lies on them.

The soul and the spirit can only be separated by the Word of God for discussion, but they actually go together. They can be distinguished, but not separated. That is why the soul has to be renewed so it can act in line with the spirit. Hebrews 4:12 says: "For the word of

God is living and powerful, and sharper than any two-edged sword, piercing even to the division of soul and spirit, and of joints and marrow, and is a discerner of the thoughts and intents of the heart."

The soul—which also includes the intellect, imagination, thoughts, will and affections—is governed by the life of the first Adam, which is a life that was corrupted by the devil in the Garden of Eden. Since mankind inherited Adam's sin nature, all of us are open to the influence of the devil.

When God created Adam, He created him whole. But because of sin the soul was damaged, and of course the spirit was too. However, when we are born again we receive a new spirit. The soul still has to be renewed with God's Word, and this is an ongoing process. Jesus came to save the spirit and repair and restore the damaged soul. Sin has had a terrible affect on the soul of man. That is where all of the problems of man originate. Because sin is so horrible, you can see why a lot of things happen in the world. Genesis 6:5 (this is after the fall of Adam.): "Then the LORD saw that the wickedness of man was great in the earth, and that every intent of the thoughts of his heart was only evil continually." People have always had a problem doing right because they are led by fallen man—sin nature. Even though they may become Christians, if they do not yield themselves to the Word, they are still going to walk as fallen man—wicked, evil, and doing anything their minds can think of to do. That is why we see a lot of wrongdoing in churches today.

You hear people say a lot of time, "Well, I thought that because they were Christians..." You have to grow in the grace and knowledge of the Lord Jesus Christ. Many believers never grow. They do not have anything to grow by because they never go where they can hear the Word that will teach them how they are to live. We understand why people in the world do all kinds of evil things and think nothing about it, but it is very sad to see Christians doing the same evil things and acting the same way.

In Romans 1:18–32, you can read some of the things mankind had come to and where people are still having a lot of problems. Romans 1:21 says, "Although they knew God, they did not glorify Him as God, nor were thankful, but became futile in their thoughts, and their foolish hearts were darkened." The word *futile* means "to make empty, vain, foolish, useless, confused." The word describes the perverted logic and idolatrous presumption of those who do not honor God or show Him any gratitude for His blessings on humanity. That verse says, "Their foolish hearts were darkened." *Vine's Dictionary* says, "The heart is the seat of one's personal life, both physical and spiritual, the center of one's personality; the seat of one's entire mental and moral activity."[1] (It sounds like the soul, doesn't it?) It is the seat of feelings, desires, joy, pain, and love. It is also the center for thoughts, understanding, and will. The heart is the dwelling place of God: the Father, the Son, and the Holy Spirit. That is why we say that we receive Jesus into our *hearts*.

Because of what Jesus has done, we should not be walking in the old nature—fallen man—because He has made us alive to walk with Him, if we choose to.

> And you He [referring to Jesus] made alive, who were dead in trespasses and sins, in which you once walked according to the course of this world, according to the prince of the power of the air, the spirit who now works in the sons of disobedience, among whom also we all once conducted ourselves in the lusts of our flesh, fulfilling the desires of the flesh and of the mind, and were by nature children of wrath, just as the others. But God, who is rich in mercy, because of His great love with which He loved us, even when we were dead in trespasses, made us alive together with Christ (by grace you have been saved), and raised us up together, and made us sit together in the heavenly places in Christ Jesus.
>
> —EPHESIANS 2:1–6

It is all up to us. But what are we supposed to do? We have to do what the Word says in Romans 12:1–2. We have to present our bodies as a living sacrifice. So many Christians don't want to do that, so they are going to be messing up until they die.

I was talking with my housekeeper, who is from El Salvador, and she was telling me what some of her people were saying about a well-known television evangelist who, some years ago, was exposed for sexual immorality. It was very sad because here he was a minister, teaching and preaching the Word all over the world for a lot of years, yet he had this problem that he obviously never dealt with. My housekeeper said, "There were just thousands of people who turned away from God because of what happened with this man. They didn't want to go to church anymore or have anything to do with God." As the body of Christ, we must be very careful to get our souls in line with God's Word. And we can do it; we just have to make up our minds to do what is right. It is simply a choice we make—a statement that "I will" or "I will not."

The sacrifice part is where you sacrifice the sex, drinking, smoking, and all the other ungodly things you used to do. You don't have to sacrifice your health, certain material things, or certain legitimate pleasures like some churches tell people to do. The sacrifice is denying your body the things it used to do that are against the Word. That is the sacrifice God wants you to make.

Another part of the soulish area is our emotions. If we are not careful, they can be another trap Satan sets for us to get us all tangled up when we are trying to move ahead in the things of God. The emotions are feelings of pain, distress, grief, fears, excitement, and affections, just to name a few that are common to man. We have happy emotions, like when a child is born or there is a birthday celebration. There are sad ones, too, such as when abuse or rejection happens. People go through abuse all the time, and there are churches full of people who have been abused in the past but are still suffering from it because they have not learned how to give it to God. If you are suffering from a past abuse (sexual, physical, or verbal), you are going to have to make a conscious effort to give that to the Lord. I know that it is not easy, but the Bible says we are to cast our care upon the Lord. (See 1 Peter 5:7.) That is what you have to do; forgive them, then give them to God and do your best to move on, free of that bondage. If you need help in dealing with a situation like abuse, there are Christian professional counselors who can be of help. Don't be ashamed to ask for such help if you need it.

Pray and believe God to lead you to the right spirit-filled Christian counselor.

If you continually allow things to upset you emotionally, it can lead to low self-esteem or even health problems. I could have allowed poor self-esteem to get me down, but, thank God, I came from loving parents who taught us about Jesus. By the time I reached my teen years, what counted most with me was loving the Lord. I came from a very poor family. There were twelve children in the family, and there was never enough of anything. There were never enough clothes. When I went to school, I would have to wear my dresses at least two or three days a week. Some of the other kids in school would laugh at me. When there were birthday parties, I was never invited because they knew I could not bring any presents. I went to school with a lot of lawyers' and doctors' kids, and they all had beautiful clothes. I hardly had anything to wear. I was taught to be clean, and I would fix myself up as best I could. But it never really bothered me; I have never been a jealous or envious person. I admired the other girls and their pretty clothes, but I didn't really envy them.

When my sister got married, she was able to have some nice clothes. She would let me wear some of them when I was in high school, but I really was into the Lord, so I didn't really give much thought to what was going on in school with the other kids. At lunchtime, while the other kids would be eating and fellowshiping, I would go to the little Bible study that was held in one of the classrooms. I was always seeking and searching for God. I know He is the reason that I am where I am today, but also because Fred and I made the commitment to follow the Word and apply it to our lives. We did what we were supposed to do.

If you want to be rich, then you have to learn to give. Luke 6:38 says: "Give, and it will be given to you: good measure, pressed down, shaken together, and running over will be put into your bosom. For with the same measure that you use, it will be measured back to you." Fred and I have given and given and given, and there is no end to how blessed we are. But it is because we wanted to please God first, and the riches followed. Serving Him has certainly paid off for us, and it will do the same for you.

God has promised to always be with us. We are really never alone.

> Let your conduct be without covetousness; be content with such things as you have. For He Himself has said, "I will never leave you nor forsake you. So we may boldly say: "The Lord is my helper; I will not fear. What can man do to me?"
> —HEBREWS 13:5–6

This is one scripture you need to teach your children so that they know they can call on Jesus any time, any place. He is and will be there to help them. He promised it. Psalm 27:10 says: "When my father and my mother forsake me, then the LORD will take care of me." You have to rely on that. You have to know that God is more real than you are, and He wants to be a real Father to you. He is the One who created us. He is the One who created the world, so you know He has to be more real than we are.

Dealing With the Soulish Area of the Mind

I read in my Spirit-filled Bible notes where it said that the word *mind* means, "A thinking through. It connotes: understanding, insight, meditations, reflections, perceptions, the gift of apprehension, the faculty of thoughts. When this faculty is renewed by the Word of God, the whole mindset changes from the spiritual negativism of the carnal man to the vibrant, God-like thinking of the spirit man." Because of what Jesus has done for us, we should not want to walk anymore in the soulish or carnal man, but in the spirit. Ephesians 2:1–6 tell us that God made us alive to Him, saved us, delivered us, and now we are seated at His right hand with Jesus. What a wonderful Father we have.

Another part of our soulish area that we have to deal with is our desires. Out of our desires come wishing, wanting, sexual desires, carnal desires, bodily appetite, lusts, cravings, and coveting. These are areas where a lot of Christians get hung up because they do not remember that the soul and the body are not saved.

I want to throw something out here because Christians need to deal with it: sexual desires should only be fulfilled in marriage. God is not blessing sexual relationships with boyfriends or girlfriends. I'm sorry, but that is just the way it is. And it doesn't matter what you think about it—whether you feel you can't do without sex or not. There are just too many Christians who go around having sex just like people in the world do. You can control yourself. You are more than body and soul. You are spirit, soul, and body. First Corinthians 6:18–20 tells us to:

> Flee [that means run from] sexual immorality. Every sin that a man does is outside the body, but he who commits sexual immorality sins against his own body. Or do you not know that your body is the temple of the Holy Spirit who is in you, whom you have from God, and you are not your own? For you were bought at a price; therefore glorify God in your body and in your spirit, which are God's.

When you become a Christian, your body does not belong to you. It belongs to God, and you have to obey Him through His Word. You can do it. God would not tell you to do something that you could not do. You feel like you can't because you have not taken time to build up your spirit man. When you do, the spirit can direct your soul, and your soul can direct your body correctly. If you don't do that, you will go down to the level of how you feel and what your body desires, even though you are born-again and love the Lord all of your life.

I have heard about so many Christians who are in these sexual relationships that just can't wait on God to do things His way. The thing that is most interesting to me is that there are some intelligent women—some are even doctors, lawyers, and other professionals—who are bringing guys into their homes and are living with them in open sin. Then they pray to God asking Him to make the guy want to marry them or to make things right. It is never going to be right the way they are living. I think most of the time we get into trouble because we won't wait on God, even people in my church who know better because they have been taught what God has to say about fornication. Every time you look around, someone is getting pregnant who is not married. Some have gotten pregnant two or three times out of wedlock. Christians! You can't go by somebody going to church and think they have it all together. These people have allowed their emotions to go down to the level of their bodies. But God told us what to do about it, and again, He will not tell us to do something we cannot do. If you don't do His Word, you will suffer the consequences.

Sometimes women get these "boyfriends" who will not even work, and the women take care of them financially. Eventually—unless she is totally not thinking right—she gets tired of the situation, and asks him to move out. Usually that is the end of the relationship, and then she is back where she started.

I heard about a situation where a female college professor was living with this man. She got tired of the guy living off her, not working and not bringing any money into the house. When she tried to do something about it, all hell broke loose. He got worse. He felt like he had a right to be there because he had been there for so long. God has better for you. You are a child of the King. Why do you take that kind of abuse? She is a beautiful woman, but she just could not control her emotions or her body, and look what she got.

Most of the time, it is not that women need sex as much as it is that they just feel the need to be loved. I have heard some women say, "I just want to be touched." You have to understand, you are not getting love; you are getting lust. Psalm 37:4 says, "Delight yourself in the Lord, and He will give you the desires of your heart." God is not a liar. If we don't do things the Bible way, we are going to suffer.

So the woman got rid of the guy, or rather he got rid of her. (That is what men do sometimes. They take advantage of you, and then when you have had enough, they just go off to another conquest.) She had other men, too, before this guy came along, but they messed up also. She went on the internet—that is how desperate some women get to find a guy—and met a man. She went with him for about two years, but he would not marry her either. Some women put up with all kinds of abuse, and all the while their souls are getting worse and worse because of the mistreatment they receive from guys who just were not right for them. Once you start doing stuff to try to make things work, the more frustrated you become and the unhappier with your life you will be. God doesn't want you going through all that. If you will get busy serving Him and looking to Him for your peace and joy, you will be so much better off than going from man to man trying to find the love you think you need. Make God the love of your life, and before you know it, He will bring into your life what He knows you need.

Ambitious Desires

Other parts of our soulish area are other traits, such as ambition, status-seeking, social climbing, and the hunger for power. It is okay to have these desires, but not to the point of walking over your brothers and sisters in the Lord. Sadly, there is too much of that in the church. People want to have power or authority, especially over others. We ought to have power, but we don't need a special job or position to get noticed. Let God put you in a particular position so you won't be fighting or promoting jealousy or envy and strife in the body of Christ.

God has told you what to do, so you don't have to go down to the level of being over-ambitious, power seeking, and power hungry. God has blessed and given special talents to men and women in the ministry—and many are doing wonderfully well—but some are just never satisfied. They always want even more power. That is why you hear about some ministers of the gospel who have done great work and they fall just before reaching the finish line. That is because the more power they get, the more power they want. The Bible tells us that promotion comes from God and we don't have to step on people to get what we want. (See

Psalm 75:6–7.) God will do it, if we have a heart to do His work.

We should love our brothers and sisters and let everybody work with the talents and gifts they have. We don't have to be pushing, shoving, and running over people just so we can get what we want, without regard for others. The pastor can see you. You don't need to do things to attract attention to yourself. If God has that job or position for you, no one can take it from you. Psalm 84:11 says, "No good thing will He withhold From those who walk uprightly."

How do you have a prosperous soul? Only by applying and being obedient to God's Word. If you are involved in all that other negative stuff I talked about, you are not being obedient to God's Word. As a result, your soul is not prospering, and you will always be a problem and have problems.

We always have to keep in mind and before our eyes that our souls are not yet saved. A lot of churches teach about "saving souls," but it should be saving *spirits*, because only the spirit gets saved at the new birth. You have to work on your soul. Changing the soul's actions and thinking is a gradual, ongoing process. We can see this in James 1:21–22:

> Therefore lay aside all filthiness and overflow
> of wickedness, and receive with meekness the
> implanted word, which is able to save your souls.
> But be doers of the word, and not hearers only,
> deceiving yourselves.

So you see, your soul can only be saved by the Word as you apply the Word. If you do not apply the Word to certain areas of your life, you will never grow in those areas. If you want your soul to prosper, you will have to do what Luke 21:19 says to: "By your patience possess your souls." It is going to take patience and your working to control your thinking and your actions on a daily basis. As you continue working the Word, you will gain more and more control over your emotions, feelings, and your mind.

If you want to be in the perfect will of God, you are going to have to deny yourself some things that you used to do—that as a Christian, you can no longer do. Jesus said in Luke 9:23, "If anyone desires to come after Me, let him deny himself, and take up his cross daily, and follow Me." It doesn't mean that you have to deny yourself all of the good things of life, but you will have to deny yourself all of the pleasures of sin—all those things you used to do that are lustful and feel good for a season. Those are the things you have to sacrifice and deny yourself.

You can be free of anything that is hindering you and keeping you down spirit, soul, and body, as well as mentally, physically, and financially. God has a word for you—just take the time to study the Scriptures and find that word that applies to your situation and then do it. We can only prosper and be in health as our soul prospers. It is up to us to see that our souls prosper. All the Lord wants you to do is to come to Him in faith and trust. Take His yoke upon you and learn of Him, for He has the answers you need.

CHAPTER 7

WHAT'S ON
YOUR MIND?

But be transformed by the renewing of
your mind.

—ROMANS 12:2

YOUR MIND—THE WAY YOU THINK—HAS a lot
to do with the quality of your life. Proverbs 23:7
says, "For as he thinks in his heart, so is he." What you
keep your mind on will determine whether you will be
at peace or whether you will be full of anxiety in this
troubled world.

Philippians 4:6–8 tells us:

Be anxious for nothing, but in everything by
prayer and supplication, with thanksgiving, let
your requests be made known to God.

—PHILIPPIANS 4:6

If you do what this verse says, then the next verse will come into play:

> And the peace of God, which surpasses all understanding, will guard your hearts and minds through Christ Jesus.
>
> —PHILIPPIANS 4:7

And the way you keep from being anxious for nothing is by doing what verse 8 says.

> Finally, brethren, whatever things are true, whatever things are noble, whatever things are just, whatever things are pure, whatever things are lovely, whatever things are of good report, if there is any virtue and if there is anything praiseworthy—meditate [constantly think] on these things.
>
> —PHILIPPIANS 4:8

So, what are you thinking about? The word *think* means "to consider, reflect, reason, and ponder."[1] What we think is what we become. Where we have kept our minds is where we are. Our thoughts shape our behavior. In other words, what we do is what we think. William Barclay, a Christian writer, says: "It is a law of life that if a man thinks on something often enough and long enough, he will come to the stage when he cannot stop thinking about it. His thoughts will be quite literally in a groove out of which he cannot jerk them."[2] How many people have gotten into bad situations because they just kept thinking and thinking and thinking about it until they found themselves in a mess. What are you thinking about? Are you thinking righteous or unrighteous thoughts? Are you thinking:

1. about the flesh and its lusts? Are you thinking about gratifying the flesh through such things as pride, self, greed, pleasure, sex, angry exchanges, jealousies, envies, desires, and negative attitudes?

2. about the lusts of the eyes through such things as immoral pornographic filth flaunted in magazines, films, books, television, and clothes that reveal too much of the body in a vulgar way?

3. about the desire for recognition, honor, position, and power? It is okay to want to be recognized, but not to the extent that you will do anything for recognition, to the extent of committing a sin or hurting someone to get what you want.

A mind fixated on the world system and the flesh is what leads to anxiety, worry, emptiness, and restlessness.

> If then you were raised with Christ, seek those things which are above, where Christ is, sitting at the right hand of God. Set your mind on things above, not on things on the earth.
>
> —COLOSSIANS 3:1–2

Setting your mind on things above means setting your mind on the things of God, and you find out about the things of God from His Word. You have to take control of your mind and make it do what it should do by a determination of your will. Your will is in the mind area.

Romans 12:1–2 tells us what to do with our minds and with our flesh.

> I beseech you therefore, brethren, by the mercies of God, that you present your bodies a living sacrifice, holy, acceptable to God, which is your reasonable service. And do not be conformed to this world, but be transformed by the renewing of your mind, that you may prove what is that good, and acceptable and perfect will of God.

I know we can renew our minds, but we have to be forever thinking about God and His great love for mankind. Because if you don't, you will think more in line with the world than with the things of God. You have to understand that the body always wants to gratify the flesh. You have to train the body, make it do what your spirit wants, kill it, sacrifice it. And sacrifice is not fun, but it is the joy of the Lord you want.

Ephesians 4:21–24 says:

> If indeed you have heard Him and have been taught by Him, as the truth is in Jesus: that you put off, concerning your former conduct, the old man which grows corrupt according to the deceitful lusts, and be renewed in the spirit of your mind, and that you put on the new man which was created according to God, in true righteousness and holiness.

It is our responsibility to do something about our minds. Once a person has been converted and becomes a new man, he is to focus his thoughts on God, as well as the good things of life. We, as believers, should never dwell on immoral, fleshly, worldly, selfish, sinful, or evil thoughts. Sinful and negative thoughts disrupt and destroy our peace. The mind always goes down to the level of the flesh, but we have to control it because we live in the flesh and that is the thing we gravitate to. And that is why we need to operate in the Word of God in order to control our thinking, which will control our flesh.

Memorize these scriptures, because if you stay with God you can train yourself to keep your mind on the things of God, and then you won't go down to the level of your mind and your flesh. Second Timothy 1:7 says: "For God has not given us a spirit of fear, but of power and of love and of a sound mind." We have a sound mind. Therefore, we have to think about the things of God, so we can think right thoughts.

"I don't think I'm ever going to get a husband." This is what I hear a lot of times from women around the church. You will get a husband if you do what God's Word says. You don't want to get the wrong husband. Too many people get the wrong mates.

I know a young lady who used to do some work for me. She came here from another country. She said she helped her husband come here, and when he got here, he dumped her. All he wanted to do was to get to America. She met another man whom she lived with for a while, but he ended up taking advantage of her too. So she ended up alone again. This girl was in the world, but Christian women go through the same thing.

My heart really goes out to single women if they are not enjoying their Christian life. I wish they could just believe God and know how much He loves them and wants to help them. However, they have to spend time with the Father and build a relationship with Him in order to develop that confidence to know He will give them the desires of their hearts if they will delight themselves in Him.

A while after she told me her story, the young lady came to see me and told me that she had met another guy. She said, "Oh, I was just so lonely." I told her, "I can imagine that it is lonely being by yourself, and I am happy that you have met someone. I hope it will be a good relationship. But whatever you do, don't sleep with him." Every time she had sex with these guys, she would feel just so bad and depressed when they would end up leaving her. This is what she said to me: "But you have to sleep with them before you marry them; otherwise, how are you going to know everything is going to work?"

I said, "Well, Adam didn't sleep with Eve. This is where you have to trust God. If you trust in your own thinking, you can get the wrong person, and you are going to get hurt over and over again." Many women have experienced this over and over again. It just breaks my heart to see women go through things like this and still end up with the wrong person or alone. They are left with the worst self-esteem, just because some man has put them down. I tell women I counsel with: "You have to know you are complete in Jesus. You don't need a man to make you complete, and you don't need a man to meet your needs because the Word says, "And my God shall supply all your need according to His riches in glory by Christ Jesus" (Phil. 4:19). If we would learn to really trust God, we could have such a beautiful life. However, if you are not committed to staying in the Word, you are going to be led by your mind, your feelings, and your body. If you think the things God tells us to think, you will be on your way because He is the most important One to please, and if you please Him, you will end up pleasing yourself and everybody else around you. If the ones who are not pleased leave you because you are with the Lord, it is OK. You do not need them around you any way.

The things listed in Philippians 4:8 are where we should be giving our attention. For example, *whatever things are true*—that means whatever things are real and genuine. Not just whatever is the truth. For instance, we don't want to dwell on a situation where a man ran off with another man's wife. That may be true, but that is not noble, honorable, or praiseworthy. No, we want to think on things highly respected, revered, and that have the dignity of holiness on them. When we say *whatever things are just*, that has to do with right behavior towards God and man.

Whatever things are pure means that what you are thinking on is morally spotless, stainless, chaste, unde-filed, and free from moral pollution, filth, dirt and impurities. You have to will to think on these things. *Whatever things are lovely* refers to those things that are pleasing, winsome, kind, gracious—things that encourage love and kindness. Our thoughts as believers should not be thoughts of meanness, grum-bling, murmuring, and criticism. We have too much of that in the body of Christ. Our thoughts are to be focused on things that are lovely, that build people up and not tear them down.

Whatever things are of good report are reputable, worthy of the highest quality.

We believers should not fill our minds with junk, gossip, envy, strife, jealousy, and evil speaking. Only that which is of good report. If there is any virtue, excel-lence, and anything praiseworthy—we are to think on these things. You need to memorize Philippians 4:8 so that when you are tempted to say something you don't have any business saying, even though it may be true, don't say it if it is not lovely and it is not of a good report. I am so sensitive to what comes out of my mouth that if I say the wrong thing I will immediately ask for forgiveness. I don't want anything to be between me and God.

I know some people think that being a Christian has to be the most boring life there is. They are so wrong. It is a wonderful life. I have been a Christian all of my life, and I have not regretted a moment of it. I have had some hard times, but it was not because I was a Christian. It was because I was ignorant and did not know what God said in His Word.

Psalm 119:11 says, "Your Word I have hidden in my heart, That I might not sin against you." If you have His Word in your heart and you are cleansed by the Word, you can make right decisions. You can have right thinking. Psalm 119:105 says, "Your word is a lamp to my feet And a light to my path." It is a wonderful thing that we have all the answers that we need in God's Word in order to live the victorious, overcoming life.

The Apostle Paul wrote the book of Philippians, and in it he is telling us to have joy and to rejoice in the Lord always. He is the one who tells us to be anxious for nothing and that the peace of God would be in our hearts through Christ Jesus if we would train ourselves to put our trust in God and not to be anxious or upset. (See Philippians 4:6–7.) If you know anything about Paul's life, he had gone through a lot of adversity, including being put in jail. In fact, he was in jail when he wrote Philippians. He was telling Christians to rejoice because we know God. Yes, we will have negative things come against us, but the joy of the Lord is our strength and He will take us through whatever we are facing. Christians are expected to control and discipline our minds, and we can do it. We are to stand against all sinful and negative thoughts and will to think only righteous thoughts. You may think, "How in the world can you think righteous thoughts all the time?" You have to will to. I can get pricked in my heart right away, even if I try to think of something evil. Satan does have access to our minds, so everything we think may not be coming from our own thinking. But the important thing is not to obey the thought. It is not what comes to your mind that is a sin; it is what you do with the thought that allows sin to come in.

Romans 8:5 says: "For those who live according to the flesh set their minds on the things of the flesh, but those who live according to the Spirit, the things of the Spirit."

Again, we are the ones who decide to set our minds on the flesh or on the Spirit, depending on whatever results you want. You can enjoy the passing pleasures of sin (Hebrews 11:25), but that is just what it is—the fleshly pleasures of sin for a season. But if you set your mind on the Spirit, then you will have the blessings of the Spirit that come from God.

Second Corinthians 10:4–5 tells us:

> For the weapons of our warfare are not carnal but mighty in God for pulling down strongholds, casting down arguments and every high thing that exalts itself against the knowledge of God, bringing every thought into captivity to the obedience of Christ.

I love these scriptures; these you need to memorize. Paul is again telling us that when thoughts come to our minds that we know are against the knowledge of God—that is, the Word of God—we are to immediately reject them. In other words, don't dwell on these unholy thoughts or give them any credit. For example, when your body is telling you that you are sick, you reject that thought and counteract it with a confession of faith: "I believe that I am healed because with Jesus' stripes I am healed. God sent His Word and healed me, and no weapon formed against me will prosper."

This is how you "cast down" those thoughts. Your confession of faith in God's Word is what you believe, not what you see or what your feel. Now I am not saying what you see or what you feel is not real, and I am surely not saying for you not to go to the doctor or ignore symptoms that you see or feel. However, you want to believe what the Bible says about healing and then do whatever it takes to take care of the symptoms in your body. This is hard to do, especially because we are governed by our bodily feelings, but you can train yourself to not dwell on or talk about how you feel, but rather talk about what the Word says about your healing. Otherwise, if you go down to the level of how you feel, that is how the enemy can end up taking you out of here.

Isaiah 26:3 says: "You will keep him in perfect peace, whose mind is stayed on You." It is up to us to keep our minds stayed on the Lord by keeping our minds stayed on the Word. If we do this, He says He will keep us in perfect peace. I love that. I would rather have the peace of God than any of the world's fame and good fortune, which only bring happiness for a moment. I would much rather be what God says to be, instead of trying to be something that I am not. Being something you are not takes a lot of effort and work, and you do not accomplish very much in the end anyway. Set your mind on the things that you want to do in life that are in line with God's Word, and with God's help you can reach your goals. When those evil thoughts come and tell you that you cannot achieve your goal, know that it is from the devil and cast that thought down.

What About Problem Thoughts?

We should not dwell on things that cause depression and real sadness, such as the death of a loved one, past mistreatment and abuse by a mate, persecution, and disappointments. Yes, these are a part of life, but we have to know that life goes on, and we have to go on too. We can't just give up, throw our hands up in the air, and say, "Well, that's it. I can't go any further."

In September 2001, we experienced a tremendous loss with the attack on America through the terrorist bombing of the Twin Towers. A lot of people didn't know what to do, and many people thought God was the cause of the problem. If we think God is our problem, how are we ever going to get out of the way of trouble? That is why you had better know what God's Word says when you come under such a heavy attack as we experienced on September 11. Those of us who know the Lord know that He is not our problem, but our solution. We need to pray for those people who do not know the Lord. We know that the death of a loved one in the Lord is not the end because the Bible says in 2 Corinthians 5:8, "To be absent from the body [is] to be present with the Lord." We don't have to be worried about them; they are doing fine. Yes, we will miss them; that is only normal. But we have to know that they are in a better place.

Revelations 14:13 says, "Blessed are the dead who die in the Lord.... that they may rest from their labors."

Psalm 116:15 tells us that, "Precious in the sight of the Lord Is the death of His saints." We should be able to minister to those who have lost a loved one, as well as minister to ourselves when a loved one—family member or friend—goes to be with the Lord. It is not that we are not going to miss that person and won't cry when they are gone, because even Jesus wept when Lazarus died. But we have to think logically and not act like those who have no hope.

I went through a great sadness when my oldest sister died. We were very close, and in many ways she was like a mother to me. She wasn't sick or anything. Her death was very painful for me, but I had to do what God's Word said do. I know she is in the presence of God and would not want to come back even if she could. She had lived a good life and lived her promised years, but I selfishly wanted her to stay here so we could have more time together. She went to be with the Lord, and then her husband followed a short time later. They had been married fifty-four years. Even though I missed them very much, I had to let them go. I could think about them being gone and be very sad, but it did not and will not help. I just thank God that we will all be together again and there will never be any more separations.

When we experience a death in the family, we can't go down to the level of where we are so depressed we can't even move and make decisions. We have to make up our minds that we have to let them go. We might feel like crying; go ahead and cry, get through it and move on, and do the work of God until your time comes. That is the thing I've decided to do. Those who got killed in the terrorist attacks who did not know God—we just have to leave them in the hands of God, knowing that He is a righteous God and He will do what is right. We don't know how many opportunities they may have had to hear about Christ and to receive Him. The Lord is not going to do anything wrong when we leave them with Him.

Jesus Is Always With Us

You have to believe what God has said and act like it is true, which it is. Some people think that prayer is just a ritual. Like when I pray every Sunday morning before the congregation. I pray the same prayer each time and some people have actually memorized it. They think, *"Doesn't she know anything else?"* I specifically pray that prayer on Sunday mornings; I also pray it everyday, because it covers everything I believe for myself, my family, and for our congregation.

Let your conduct [your manner of living or life-
style] be without covetousness [greed for gain];
be content with such things as you have. For
He Himself has said, "I will never leave you nor
forsake you." So we may boldly say: "The Lord
is my helper; I will not fear. What can man do
to me?"

—HEBREWS 13:5–7

If you know that God has said He will never leave
you nor forsake you, what do you have to fear? Every
day I say, "Jesus is our Lord and Savior. He is our healer,
our deliverer, our coming King, our advocate, our high
priest, our intercessor, our provider, our protector, our
friend, and He will never leave us nor forsake us." That
way, whenever I get into a situation, I know Jesus is
with me. He will never leave me, nor forsake me. I can't
see Him because He is in the spirit world. The spirit
world is more real than this physical world, because
the spirit world created this world. The angels are with
me, so I don't worry that anything will harm me. This
keeps me at peace all the time. When I pray, I am not
just saying words; I believe what I am saying.

Prayer is a set time with God for devotion, petition,
and intercession. We should be praying and spending
time with God every day. You should have a set time
that you meet with Him. That is how you get to know

Him. That is how you can be conscious of Him at all times. Your mind can stay on Him at all times. If your mind is on God, it will not go back to the times that you spent with an old girlfriend or boyfriend and the way you used to be, those times when you had those candles burning and your romantic music playing in a darkened room. You can't think on that kind of stuff. You have to be thinking about the goodness of God, because if you don't, you are going to go down to the level of the flesh and the way you used to be in sin.

The Apostle Paul tells us in Philippians 4:6 that we are not to be anxious or concerned about anything, but by prayer and supplication we are to make our requests known to God.

Supplication is more than just petitioning God or asking God for something. It means a high degree of intensity of earnest and extended prayer. Sometimes certain things will stay with you longer (which is what we believers describe as, "having a burden for prayer"), so you stay in prayer supplicating, or praying in the Spirit and bringing God's Word before Him. He knows His Word, but we need to remind ourselves what His Word promises. Paul says that when we do this, "The peace of God, which surpasses all understanding, will guard your hearts and minds through Christ Jesus" (Phil. 4:7).

The King James Version of the Bible uses the word *keeps* and the New King James Version uses the word *guards*, but they both mean the same thing. That word *guard* is a military term, picturing a sentry standing guard as protection against the enemy. We are in spiritual combat, but God's power and peace are our sentinels and protection. That is why you need to pray, spend time with God, and get to know Him. A lot of preachers think that we who teach faith—those who are in the Faith movement—say that Christians don't have to go through struggles, trials, or tests. They have never heard the whole message on faith, because with all the things we have been through we have never said that. No, the thing that we teach is that we don't center on the trials and tests, but we center on the truth: "But the LORD delivers him out of them all" (Ps. 34:19).

I focus on the deliverance part, not the going-through part. I refuse to be anxious or worried because I know God is going to bring me through. You are going to have to make up your mind that you are going to believe God. The greatest thing you can do in life is to learn to walk by faith and not by sight. (See 2 Corinthians 5:7.)

Luke 18:1 says, "Then He spoke a parable to them, that men always ought to pray and not lose heart." We should always pray, but that does not mean to pray twenty-four hours a day—it means don't ever give up the avenue of prayer.

John 15:7 says that "if you abide in Me, and My words abide in you, you will ask what you desire, and it shall be done for you." You have to have a relationship with Jesus so that you know He will do what He says. He says you can ask what you will. That is a big promise. Why don't you take Jesus at His word and prove Him. I have, and I know He can be counted on to fulfill His promises.

> Now this is the confidence that we have in Him, that if we ask anything according to His will, He hears us. And if we know that He hears us, whatever we ask, we know that we have the petitions that we have asked of Him.
>
> —1 JOHN 5:14–15

You have to get into the Word to find out what His revealed will is. His Word covers everything you need in life to live a successful, victorious, and overcoming life.

I want you to know that you have a God who loves you, has given His life for you, and He wants the very best for you. I am a living witness of the goodness of God. He has brought me from sickness to health, from poverty to wealth, and He can and will do the same for you, for He is no respecter of persons.

CHAPTER 8

HOW TO DEAL
WITH YOUR ISSUES

For out of the heart spring the issues of life.
—PROVERBS 4:23, AUTHOR'S PARAPHRASE

P ROVERBS 4:20–27 GIVES US SOME very sound
advice if we want to move ahead with God:

My son [that includes daughters as well], give
attention to my words; Incline your ear to my
sayings. Do not let them depart from your eyes;
Keep them in the midst of your heart; For they
are life to those who find them, and health to
all their flesh. Keep your heart with all diligence
[that is careful effort, perseverance], For out of
it spring the issues of life. Put away from you a
deceitful mouth, And put perverse lips far from
you. Let your eyes look straight ahead, And your
eyelids look right before you. Ponder the path of
your feet, And let all your ways be established.

Do not turn to the right or the left; Remove your
foot from evil.

According to these verses, how we deal with the
issues or challenges that face us in life come from our
hearts. In the following verses, Jesus gives us some
more information about the issues that come from
the heart:

> But those things which proceed out of the mouth
> come from the heart, and they defile a man. For
> out of the heart proceed evil thoughts, murders,
> adulteries, fornication, thefts, false witness,
> blasphemies.
>
> —Matthew 15:18–19

For from within, out of the heart of men, proceed
evil thoughts, adulteries, fornications, murders, thefts,
covetousness, wickedness, deceit, lewdness, an evil
eye, blasphemy, pride, foolishness. All these evil things
come from within and defile a man.

> —Mark 7:21–23

Jesus is telling us that any time we are involved in
fornication, adultery, and all the other things He listed
in Matthew and Mark, they come out of the heart. That
is why you have to protect your heart, in order to keep
those things from getting in there.

Luke 6:45 says: "A good man out of the good treasure of his heart brings forth good; and an evil man out
of the evil treasure of his heart brings forth evil. For
out of the abundance of the heart his mouth speaks." It
is up to us as Christians to keep ugly things out of our
hearts and to protect our hearts with all diligence by
right thinking and right action. So many people bring
the types of things listed in Matthew 15 and Mark 7
from the world right into their Christian life because
they have never been told that they do not have to keep
those things in their hearts and they don't have to do
them. Many believers don't really know how to take
the Word and drive these things out of their hearts.

You might be wondering where the heart is. We know
it is on the inside of us. There are many views about
where the heart is. There are some who say the heart is
where the spirit and the soul meet. This theory witnesses
with my spirit. The Bible indicates that the *spirit man* is
the *heart of man.* The heart and the soul go together.
You can only separate them to talk about them, but they
go together. When a person gets born again, he or she is
supposed to take his or her born-again spirit—the new
man—and renew the new man's mind, by the Word of
God. The renewed mind is a part of the heart and is the
soul and spirit combined. It now exercises control over
the "old man"—the soul that used to control the heart.

How Do Issues Get Into the Heart?

These negative issues enter the heart through thoughts, ideas, and suggestions that are planted by Satan and also by the eye (what we see), the ear gates (what we hear), and by the mind (the things we experience and dwell on). Some of the other issues of the heart we also deal with, in addition to the ones Jesus talked about in Matthew and Mark are: sicknesses, bad relationships, rejection, promiscuity, hurts, depression, abuse, low self-esteem, loneliness, lying, jealousy, envy, gossip, bitterness, guilt, malice, lack of peace, lack of finances, worry, fear, excess weight, racism, prejudices, and unforgiveness. The list goes on and on. We can't cover every issue, but there is a principle that leads to victory over every one of them: *you cannot get victory over your issues or live the Christian life victoriously without the Word of God.* You can take this same principle and deal with whatever issues you may be facing. There are still too many churches today that do not teach the uncompromising Word or the word of faith. Believers who attend these churches are usually up and down in their Christian walk. They may get emotionalized every week, but they are not taught to be overcomers. That is why they live in and out of sin, committing fornication and adultery and doing all the other junk we covered earlier. Even when they are in church, they may be planning how they are going to meet their girlfriend or boyfriend and have sex that night. They may shout and fall out every Sunday morning in church, even after having a sexual affair that Saturday night before.

They are what we call *carnal Christians*, and basically they live that way because they don't know they can do better. They do not have enough Word in them. They will never have peace in their lives because they can't continue to live that kind of life and be prosperous or victorious in the kingdom of God. If you are caught in such a trap, the only way to escape and find peace is to find out what the Word says about your situation and then do what it says. What does the Word say about fornication? What does it say about adultery? You are going to have to refuse to go down to the level of how you feel, and make up your mind that you are going to do what the Bible says to do.

The feelings you may be having in your body are normal, but being normal does not mean they may be right to do. You have to take the Word and get rid of those feelings, and let God bring into your life what you need at the right time. I heard a woman say: "Well, God is just too slow and I need this relationship." I have known of women who have gone with guys for two or three years and later found out these men were already seriously involved with someone else. (I say women because most of the time it is the women who go through things like this.) God does not want you to have a meaningless relationship. He wants you to have a relationship that is meaningful. If the guy keeps telling you that he is going to marry you, but he never sets a date or even gives you a ring, after a while you should know something is very wrong.

I heard of a situation where a young lady was messing around with this guy for two years. Later, she found out that the reason he kept putting her off and would not marry her—telling her he was trying to get his finances together—was he was already married. She saw him somewhere on the street with another woman and two little kids. His wife lived in another city. This is why you need to know what and who you are dealing with and not do things apart from the Word of God.

Notice Proverbs 4:20–23 again:

> My son, give attention to my words; Incline your ear to my sayings.
>
> —PROVERBS 4:20

That means to tend to the Word, read and study it. Continue to hear the Word, because faith comes by hearing.

Do not let them depart from your eyes; Keep
them in the midst of your heart.
—Proverbs 4:21

You can't afford to take your eyes off the Word. Even
some strong Christians have taken their eyes off of the
Word and have gone down to the level of their feelings
and they found themselves messed up. You can keep
the Word in the midst of your heart by meditating on
it, thinking about it, and doing it. If you follow this
advice, I believe it will keep you from falling into those
issues and situations that will cause you misery.

For they are life to those who find them, And
health to all their flesh. Keep your heart with all
diligence, For out of it spring the issues of life.
—Proverbs 4:22–23

If you want real life, there is no life apart from Jesus
Christ or from His Word. If you don't keep or protect
your heart with all diligence, those old issues will flare
up time and time again.

We Must Give Attention to the Word

I know the story of another young woman who
attended our church years ago. The church was fairly
new, and we were just getting started moving in the

things of the Word. We had a lot of young men who started out with us, and a lot of the single women were trying to pick husbands for themselves. A couple of the women literally got into fussing and fighting over a particular man. These women ended up letting the issues of anger, strife, and jealousy get into their hearts. One lady finally admitted that she had gotten into strife with the other woman over this man. She ended up getting a serious disease, and said to me, "When I get healed, I will tell other women never to get into stress over things like this." She really wanted to be healed, but she died far too young.

I was listening to a pastor's wife when I ministered in New York at Crenshaw Christian Center East as she shared about women in the world who go on certain television shows where two or three women openly fight over the same man. It really is disgraceful to see women acting in that kind of way—fighting over a man on television, when they should be getting together and getting rid of him. He is certainly not worth it. I had a lady at our church tell me, "Well, a piece of a man is better than no man at all." She is not thinking like a Christian woman should think. If she continues to think like that, she is definitely headed for a problem, because that means she is willing to settle for any man she can get.

There are a number of women who think like that because they put so much credence into having a man. Some women stay with men all their lives knowing he has another family somewhere. They take that emotional abuse because they would rather be with any kind of man than be alone. But if they would only just know that Jesus is with them all the time, wanting the very best for them! They are not alone. I have heard of situations where a man had a couple of families in other places. I don't know how women who are married can let their husbands get away with that. If your husband is not around a lot of the time, don't you have questions about where he is when he is not with you and your children? How many jobs can a man have?

Our mouths, lips, eyes, hands, and feet are instruments of communication. Usually, we get messed up with issues that deal with these instruments, our eyes and feet going somewhere they should not be going. You have no business meeting some man in a hotel room if you are not married to him. When you do things like that, you will end up messed up.

Issues We Face on a Daily Basis

We have to deal with the issue of sickness and disease because it is a common problem for mankind. Matthew

8:17 says that "He Himself [Jesus] took our infirmities And bore our sicknesses." First Peter 2:24 says, "by [His] stripes we were healed." And Psalm 103:3 tells us that Jesus is the One "Who forgives all your iniquities, Who heals all your diseases." In case the devil tries to bring to your mind all the wrong things you have done so you can't get your healing, well, you just tell him that Jesus has forgiven you of all your iniquities (sins) and has paid the price for you to be healed of all your diseases. This is how you keep the Word before you— by speaking God's Word to the circumstances of life.

Psalm 107:20 says, "He sent His Word and healed them, And delivered them from their destructions." You are going to have to believe this Word and learn how to apply it to your life by confessing it daily by faith.

Mark 11:24 says, "Therefore I say to you, whatever things you ask when you pray, believe that you receive them, and you will have them." We can never teach on this verse too much, because there are still so many people who really do not understand how the principle of faith works. The Word of God says that when you pray you have to believe you receive what you prayed for *before* you see it. The moment you pray, you have to believe you have it. That word, *have*, is in the present tense. It takes time between the time you believe you receive it and the time you have it in the natural realm.

Your part is to believe you received when you prayed, and only then will you have it.

That is what I had to do when I was attacked with cancer. It took two years from the time I believed I received my healing and the time I had the manifestation of my healing. If you put your faith in God, He is not going to let you down, but there are some things you might have to do. There are reasons why something doesn't happen overnight. I would have liked to have experienced a miracle healing, and I would have liked for God to have healed me in an instant. But I had to go through the healing process for two years, mainly because I needed to work on myself. I needed to learn to work with the doctors. When I first went to the doctors and they told me what I needed to do, I didn't want to do it. A lot of people do that, and they leave this earth realm before their time because they didn't work with the doctors. Doctors cannot heal you, but what they can do is to give you medicine and treatments that will place your body in an environment in which the healing power of God can take place.

When some women get symptoms of breast cancer or a lump or something like that, they get afraid. Faith and fear do not work together. What these women end up doing is waiting too long to go to the doctor. If you go to the doctor the moment you get some type of symptom, more often than not, the breast cancer can be healed. But what happens is that most people don't go soon enough and the cancer spreads everywhere. We end up losing good Christians who claim they are standing in faith. They have all kinds of reasons why they don't want to go to the doctor and do what they are supposed to do, but mainly it is because they are afraid: "I don't want to lose my breast." I heard a woman say, "My husband likes my breasts." Well, he had better like you better than your breasts.

I watched other people at church who had taken the chemo and radiation, and I said to myself, "Well, if the doctors can't tell me that chemo is going to heal me, then I am not going to take it." But that was my mistake. God did not tell me do this. I did it. I waited eight months before I got help. God was merciful to me. But I can tell you—don't wait! When I finally went, the doctors told me exactly what they had told me eight months before; I needed to have chemotherapy and radiation to get rid of the tumor.

During those eight months, the tumor kept growing. As a result, I got to the place where I couldn't walk, and I had to get around in a wheelchair. But God is so good. The tumor never spread to other parts of my body, but I had to fight against all those thoughts that kept coming to my mind. I had to use the Word of God against the pain, as well as the thoughts that bombarded my mind, telling me, "You are not going to make it. You are getting worse by the day, and you are going to end up dead." I thank God for doctors. When I finally did what the doctors told me to do, and as I continued working the Word of God, I came up out of that death situation.

It may not be a healing you need right now. Maybe it's a financial situation. The principle is still the same. You can use Mark 11:24 for any situation you encounter in life. With Mark 11:24, you can believe to be delivered from financial difficulties or any other situation you may be going through. It is up to you to believe God and know that He will confirm His Word in your life.

In James 1:2–4, James tells us about the attitude we should have when we are believing for the manifestation of what we prayed to receive.

> My brethren, count it all joy when you fall into various trials, knowing that the testing of your faith produces patience. But let patience have its perfect work, that you may be perfect and complete, lacking nothing.

James tells us to, "count it all joy." Notice, he didn't say it *was* joy. He said to act like it is joy. Everyone can make this choice, because our wills are involved. I realized that I could act like what I was going through was joy, or I could go down to the level of how I really felt, which would have killed me.

Personal Issues

Relationships, rejection, hurt, promiscuity, depression, abuse, low self-esteem, loneliness, or any other personal issue you can name could overwhelm you, if you let them. There are many Christians who suffer from these issues, even though God has given us a way to get rid of that stuff. But it is up to us to apply the Word to those situations.

Most people suffer from these issues because they do not know who they are in Christ. You need to find who you are in Christ. Get into the Bible starting from Romans to Jude, and find all the words that tell you what you have in Jesus Christ. Then you need to memorize all of them. That is what I do so that when I need these scriptures they are in my spirit for me to pull from. It is up to you to do that, because there are just too many Christians who are looking for acceptance and love in the wrong places. That is why my heart hurts to see so many women suffering and going to the wrong sources to satisfy their desire for love. Christians should not have to do that, but some believers act just like people who are not Christians.

If you are searching and don't feel like you are all that you should be, these scriptures are for you:

> For in Him dwells all the fullness of the Godhead bodily; and you are complete in Him, who is the head of all principality and power.
> —Colossians 2:9–10

So ladies, you don't need a man to complete you. You need *the* Man. You need to think about Jesus and all that He has done for you. The Man is not going to take advantage of you.

> Yet in all these things we are more than conquerors through Him who loved us.
> —Romans 8:37

See yourself as more than a conqueror. Don't go down to the level of how somebody treats you, making you feel less than who you really are. Jesus Christ is the One who validates you and tells you who you are.

Other Personal Issues

Other personal issues include lying, anger, bitterness, gossip, and malice. We have to put these things off.

Ephesians 4:25 says, "Therefore, putting away lying, 'Let each one of you speak truth with his neighbor,' for we are members of one another." You have to put lying away. It is up to you. If you have some of these issues, there is no need to pray for God to take them away because God doesn't want your issues. He wants you to deal with them. Ephesians 4:26 tells us, "'Be angry, and do not sin': do not let the sun go down on your wrath." We ought to be angry about ungodly things that people do, but we need to put away anger that gets out of control and causes us not only to lose our temper but our manners and good behavior as well. Verse 27 gives us this great advice: "Nor give place to the devil." See, it is up to us to give place or not to give place to the devil. He just cannot take a place in our lives if we do not give it to him.

> Let no corrupt word proceed out of your mouth, but what is good for necessary edification, that it may impart grace to the hearers. And do not grieve the Holy Spirit of God, by whom you were sealed for the day of redemption.
>
> —EPHESIANS 4:29–30

Our ungodly actions grieve the Holy Spirit a lot of times; that is why we really need to watch what we say or what we do when we claim to represent Jesus.

Ephesians 4:31–32 is another set of scriptures we need to pay particular attention to if we want to rid ourselves of the issues that hold us back from living a disciplined Christian lifestyle and obeying God's Word:

> Let all bitterness, wrath, anger, clamor, and evil speaking be put away from you, with all malice. And be kind to one another, tenderhearted, forgiving one another, even as God in Christ forgave you.

The Issues of Envy and Jealousy

First Peter 2:1–3 tell us what to do about these issues that keep us from having God's peace in our lives:

> Therefore, laying aside all malice, all deceit, hypocrisy, envy, and all evil speaking, as newborn babes, desire the pure milk of the word, that you may grow thereby, if indeed you have tasted that the Lord is gracious.

We can do that if we know the Lord. We lay aside all that malice, envy, deceit, evil speaking, and all the other junk that continually goes on in the body of Christ. I don't understand people. Why would you be jealous of anyone because they got a new car? Why would you care where they got it from? "How did they get that car?" people ask. Well, that is none of your business. You're not paying for it. All the jealousies and all that envy going on in your head—wasting your time worrying about what someone else has and the gifts and talents they have. God expects you to use what you have. He is the only One that you have to please. You can't be looking at somebody else.

Keep your eyes straight ahead. Do what you are supposed to do. If you are not looking at somebody else, you won't know what they are doing and you will not have to be tempted to be jealous of them. You can't do anything about what they have anyway. If they are gifted, you can't do anything about it. You can't take their gift—God gave it to them. If they are beautiful, you can't do anything about that because you can't take the beauty God gave to them. If they have a whole lot of hair and I wish I had a lot of hair, I am not going to be jealous of somebody else's hair because I can't get it. It doesn't pay to be jealous and envious of anybody because you can't get what they have. All you do is make yourself miserable and you could get into sin. It must be horrible to be always concerned about what somebody else has. You can save yourself a lot of energy, strength, worry, and unhappiness if you make the effort to avoid being envious.

Proverbs 16:7 says, "When a man's ways please the Lord, He makes even his enemies to be at peace with him." That is a wonderful scripture to memorize. When someone does something to you and you know you are innocent of what they are holding against you, know that God has promised to make it right for you. So go on and forgive and forget. People have done a lot of things to my family and I, but we have stood strong because we know all we have to do is to be right with God. I don't care what people have done to me; I forgive them, and I say to the Lord, "God forgive them, for they know not what they do."

Now I'm not saying I am going to trust them or put myself in a position to be hurt again. If I know you have been lying on me and trying to cut my throat, I am definitely going to forgive you, but I will not place myself in your path of attack again. Some people have had to put up with a lot of situations in their lives, like mental or physical abuse, or both. However, if you are out of that situation, you can move on with your life. A part of that moving on is forgiving the other person. You can do it, because your will is involved. I don't care what people have done to you; you can still forgive so that God can continue to move in your life.

We need to follow Paul's advice in Philippians 3:13–14:

> Forgetting those things which are behind and
> reaching forward to those things which are
> ahead, I press toward the goal for the prize for
> the upward call of God in Christ Jesus.

If you have been abused by your husband or boyfriend, whatever that man has done to you, forgive him. However, don't let him stay in your life to beat up on you and mess over you. You don't have to stay in a situation like that, and God does not require you to do so. If you decide to stay in the situation, believing God to work things out, there are things you are going to have to do. You will have to be a good wife to your husband. You should be taking care of him and the children; taking care of the house, taking care of his clothes, his food, and not doing things you are not supposed to do, such as depriving your husband of sex. Sometimes when people first get married or even later, they may go through a stage of not wanting to have an intimate time with their spouses. That is very dangerous, because there are some people out there who are very willing to accommodate your husband or wife.

You need to obey the Word, because in 1 Corinthians 7:3–5 it tells the wife not to deprive the husband and the husband not to deprive the wife. You might have to grow up and learn to be intimate at the right time with your spouse. That was a challenge for me when I first got married. When Fred and I got married, I got pregnant within two months. I never had an intimate relationship before I got married, so I didn't know what sex was all about. At first I didn't want to be bothered with my husband. After I had my children, things were fine, but then I would be tired a lot of the time because there was a lot of work to do in taking care of the house and the kids. Added to all of the work, there was a lot of stress and worry because we didn't have enough money. Because we weren't in the Word at that time or going to a church that told us how not to have stress and worry, we suffered. A lot of the time, I would tell Fred, "I don't feel like it—tomorrow night," when it came to our intimate time. Then the next night would come, and I would say the same thing—"I don't feel like it."

Something told me, "You better feel like it, or you are not going to have a husband." This was one place where I used my faith. I tell this all the time because it is wonderful to really grow up in faith and learn that you can use you faith on anything. The Bible says, "We walk by faith, not by sight" (2 Cor. 5:7). That means you walk by the Word of God and not by how you feel. The Word also says for spouses not to deprive one another (1 Corinthians 7:5). To use my faith over our intimate time, I said, "Well, Lord, you are going to have to help me, because if this marriage goes wrong, I don't want to be responsible for the break up." That was before I really learned to walk by faith. I just decided that I was going to do what I was supposed to do and the feelings would come. Too many wives are waiting for the feeling, but some wives will never get to the point where they will enjoy their intimate moments with their spouse if they don't make it an act of faith first. The devil will see to it by putting all kinds of physical and mental demands on your body throughout the day. If you allow the circumstances of life to take first place you will end up too tired to enjoy your intimate time with your husband. Ladies, you need to have and enjoy your intimate moments with your husband, or that little cute co-worker with her short dresses and bosom all out may be ready to provide for his needs in that area. That is why you have to use wisdom. It doesn't have anything to do with how you feel. I didn't feel like being bothered some times, but after all these years we've learned to make dates with each other and that makes it nice for both of us.

Concerning Lack of Finances

Philippians 4:19 tells us: "And my God shall supply all your need according to His riches in glory by Christ Jesus." That is a promise from God. This is an excellent scripture to confess and stand on when you are believing for your finances to get better. But you have to also be doing what you can to give into the kingdom of God, as with giving tithes and offerings. Tithes and offerings are not just to meet the needs of the local church but are also avenues by which God can return to you a harvest from the seed sown. You can't declare that God is going to meet your need if you are not doing your part to meet the needs He is concerned about. His way of meeting your financial needs is through your tithes and offerings. If you are not in a position to tithe—in other words, to give 10 percent of your net income to the church, according to Malachi 3:8–10—because you are a new Christian or you were not taught, you should begin giving offerings. An offering can be of any amount until you are in a financial position to tithe. Tithing is God's best financial plan for the body of Christ, and as soon as you are in a position to do so, you should become a tither.

Psalm 112:1–3 is one of my favorite scriptures, and I have raised my children on it:

> Praise the Lord! Blessed is the man who fears the LORD, Who delights greatly in His commandments. His descendents will be mighty on earth; the generation of the upright will be blessed. Wealth and riches will be in his house, And his righteousness endures forever.

You don't have to have any schemes or things like that to get wealth and riches. Just do it God's way:

> Bring all the tithes into the storehouse... And try me now in this... If I will not open for you the windows of heaven And pour out for you such blessing That there will not be room enough to receive it.
>
> —MALACHI 3:10

> Give, and it will be given to you: good measure, pressed down, shaken together, and running over will be put into your bosom. For with the same measure that you use, it will measured back to you.
>
> —LUKE 6:38

> He who sows [gives] sparingly will also reap sparingly, and he who sows bountifully will also reap bountifully.
>
> —2 CORINTHIANS 9:6

If you do these things, it will automatically work, but you have to do your part. You have to be a giver. When we were struggling those many years ago, we learned about tithing and giving, and we started doing it. We started giving 10 percent, then 12 ½ percent, then 15 percent, then 20 percent, and so on. Now we give God 40 percent of everything we get and plan to go higher. We struggled all those years because we were robbing God by not tithing and we didn't even know it. Now that we are givers, we have no financial lack whatsoever. It is absolutely an awesome life. You can't figure out how God is going to bring monies to you. You don't have to try to figure it out. Just do what He says, and He will do His part.

Right after the tragedy on September 11, the church lost more than a million dollars in revenue. We had to let some people go, and some of them were very angry, mean, and nasty about it. We didn't want to do it, but we had to in order to keep the ministry operating. I had been getting a salary, so I told my husband I wanted to give my salary back to the church. He and our daughter Angela didn't want me to do it. She said I should not do it because I liked to give money to people in need. Fred is at a stage where he can take care of me, buy my clothes, and feed me. I give away all of the money I make. I said, "Since I give my money away anyway, why can't I give it back to the church? This is the time they need the money." Anyway, they agreed and I said, "I trust God. Look at the seed and the return I will get on it." I am a living witness that these principles work. God paid me way more than the church ever paid me, just by people giving to me and sending me money. I never asked anybody for anything. I have not been down. I haven't missed a beat because God has blessed my offering and He has given back to me in abundance. You truly cannot beat God's giving. That was in September 2001, and I have not had a salary since. The church could pay me a salary now, but I told them I don't want the money back because I am receiving such wonderful returns on giving it away. It is very exciting. Your finances will get better when you are willing to give, and give generously, into the kingdom for the benefit of God's children and His work.

The Issue of Lack of Peace

Jesus said in John 14:27, "Peace I leave with you, My peace I give to you; not as the world gives do I give to you. Let not your heart be troubled, neither let it be afraid." It is up to you to not let your heart be troubled, because Jesus has given you the peace. You just have to believe it and act like you are peaceful, whether you feel like it or not. Then the peace will come. I know that doing these things are not easy, but you can train yourself to do the Word. The benefits are just absolutely wonderful.

In John 16:33, Jesus said, "That in Me you may have peace. In the world you will have tribulation; but be of good cheer, I have overcome the world." With anything that comes to bring you fear and steal your peace, remember that if you are in Jesus, He has overcome the world and is going to take care of you in all situations. You have to make up your mind to believe the Word because scary things are happening all the time: hurricanes, earthquakes, and all kinds of other disasters. How can you make it without Jesus Christ? Everything we are or hope to be is in Him. We will never have peace apart from Jesus Christ, so it is up to us to walk in that peace.

A couple of other issues I wanted to cover are worry and being overweight. Scriptures you can use to deal with anything including weight are Philippians 4:13—" I can do all things through Christ who strengthens me"—and 1 John 4:4, which promises that "He who is in you is greater than he who is in the world."

It took our daughter Angela twenty-five years to lose the weight she had put on after her marriage and the birth of her children. But during that time, she was never down or jealous of anybody else who had lost weight, even though she had tried to lose weight with only a little success. Finally she made up her mind to do it, and it took her six months to lose sixty pounds. Don't get down on yourself if you have not reached your goal. Angela is a good example of why not to give up. I don't care how hard it seems to be. Maybe it is a particular sin that you have a hard time getting over. Don't give up trying to conqueror it. Always get up and try again, no matter what it is. Never give up on your goal of what you are believing God for.

Concerning worry, do what Philippians 4:6–7 says:

> Be anxious for nothing, but in everything by prayer and supplication, with thanksgiving, let your request be made known to God; and the peace of God, which surpasses all under- standing, will guard your hearts and minds through Christ Jesus.

You can easily tell whether you are obeying that Word. If you are not anxious and are experiencing the peace of God, then you know you are obeying what the Word says.

The Issue of Fear

Isaiah 41:10 tells us: "Fear not, for I am with you; Be not dismayed, for I am your God. I will strengthen you,

Yes, I will help you, I will uphold you with My righteous right hand." What a wonderful, reassuring scripture this is. You definitely need to memorize this one. It will comfort you any time fear tries to raise its ugly head, because we know where that fear is coming from. God has reassured us again and again that He is with us and He will never leave us nor forsake us.

Then, of course, there is always 2 Timothy 1:7: "For God has not given us a spirit of fear, but of power and of love and of a sound mind." When I was tempted to be fearful, I would say over and over, "I am not afraid. I have power. I have love, and I have a sound mind." I can tell all kinds of stories of how fearful I used to be, but I am happy to say that fear no longer has any authority over me. I conquered fear many years ago, and I refuse to allow it to come up against me ever again. We have God and His promises on our side. What more do we need to conqueror anything that comes against us? How can we lose with what we have authority to use?

You can have victory over any of these issues we talked about. You know the solution lies in the Word of God, and your determination to do the Word can and will bring you success.

NOTES

Chapter 1:
Walking in the Spirit

1. This period in Dr. Betty's life is covered in detail in her book, *Through the Fire & Through the Water–My Triumph Over Cancer.*

Chapter 2:
Walking in the Flesh

1. Wilderness.net Archives, Wilderness.net Feature: Clinton Anderson, http://www.wilderness.net/index .cfm?fuse=feature1206 (accessed August 7, 2007).

Chapter 3:
Walking in the Blessings of God

1. Harvey and Marilyn Diamond, *Fit for Life* (New York: Warner Books, Inc., 1995), 123.

Chapter 5:
A Sound Heart

1. Merrill F. Unger and William White, Jr., eds., *Vine's Expository Dictionary of Biblical Words* (Nashville, TN: Thomas Nelson, 1985), 297.

Chapter 6:
A Prosperous Soul

1. Ibid.

Chapter 7:
What's on Your Mind?

1. *Merriam-Webster's Collegiate Dictionary*, 10th edition (Springfield, MA: Merriam-Webster, 1993), 226.

2. William Barclay, *The Letter to the Philippians* (Louisville, KY: Westminster Press, 1957).

ABOUT THE
AUTHOR

DR. BETTY R. PRICE IS the wife of Dr. Frederick K.C. Price, founder and pastor of Crenshaw Christian Center East in Manhattan, New York and Crenshaw Christian Center West, home of the 10,000-seat FaithDome and Ever Increasing Faith Ministries, located in Los Angeles, California. As First Lady, Dr. Betty is an integral part of her husband's ministry and travels extensively with him ministering and teaching the uncompromising Word of God.

She plays a pivotal role at Crenshaw Christian Center. Her love and concern for others have led to the establishment of numerous programs and groups at the church including:

§   Women's Fellowship, which has become
    a model for many women's auxiliaries at
    other churches.

ᔥ   Women Who Care is designed for godly women to share their expertise, experiences and testimonies to inform, inspire and encourage other women in the things of God.

ᔥ   Big Sisters/Little Sisters Program spearheaded by godly young ladies who are positive role models for other young ladies in the Body of Christ.

ᔥ   24-Hour Intercessory Prayer Network for members, visitors and friends.

ᔥ   Alcohol/Drug Abuse and Co-Dependency Programs provide a means of helping those afflicted with the scourge of drug abuse.

ᔥ   Community Outreach Program distributes food, clothing and toys to the indigent in the communities surrounding the church.

ᔥ   Encouragement and Cancer Support Group meets weekly using the Word of God to assure participants that they have the victory over cancer.

ઽ   Vermont Village Community Development Corporation, an organization established for the purpose of improving and beautifying the Vermont corridor in south-central Los Angeles and bringing viable businesses back into the community.

Drs. Fred and Betty have been married over fifty years and all but one of those years have been spent in ministry. They have four living children: Angela Marie Evans, Cheryl Ann Price, Stephanie Pauline Buchanan and Frederick Kenneth Price. All of the Price children and their sons-in-laws: A. Michael Evans, Jr. and Danon Buchanan work in the ministry. They also have one daughter-in-law, Angel Brown Price. Drs. Price have one deceased son, who was struck and killed by a car when he was only eight years of age.

A minister of the gospel and a popular guest speaker, Dr. Betty received an Honorary Doctorate degree in June 1993 from the Southern California School of Ministry, located in Inglewood, California and was ordained to the ministry in January 1994.

For more information, to receive a catalog, or to be placed on the Ever Increasing Faith Ministries mailing list, please contact:

Crenshaw Christian Center
P.O. Box 90000
Los Angeles CA 90009
(800) 927-3436

Check your local TV or Webcast listing for
Ever Increasing Faith Ministries
or visit our Web site: www.faithdome.org

MORE BOOKS BY DR. BETTY R. PRICE

Through the Fire & Through the Water:

My Triumph Over Cancer

In 1990, Dr. Betty laid in her hospital bed under a possible sentence of death. But she heard words of life in her spirit—"This illness is not unto death, but that the Son of God may be glorified through it." Dr. Betty and the Price family share the story of her battle.

1-883798-33-7: English

(Also, available in Spanish and audio-book)

Lifestyles of the Rich & Faithful

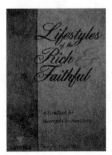

A Handbook for Successful Christian Living

In this book Dr. Betty candidly explores the challenges faced by many Christians today in handling perplexing problems that are hindering them from receiving the promised blessings of God.

1-883798-40-X

Standing by God's Man

It definitely takes a lot of grace—God's grace—not only to be a preacher's wife, but to be a Christian wife. This book chronicles Dr. Betty's testimony of her early years and is a recipe to supporting and living with a great man of God.
1-599790-49-3 (Mini-book)

These teachings are also available on CD and Cassette. For the latest information on other books, visual and audio products please contact us at:

(800) 927-3436
www.faithdome.org

MOST RECENT AUDIO RELEASES BY DR. BETTY R. PRICE

Wisdom From Above

These six teachings by Dr. Betty specifically speak to the Issues that plague so many Christian women and how to Overcome the issues of life through God's Word. This wealth of wisdom includes: What's On Your Mind?, Making Wise Choices, How to Deal With Your Issues and much more.
BPD 8 (6-CD)

Healing Is Our Covenant Right

Is it God's will for Christians to suffer in sickness and disease? Your church may say it is, but what does God's Word say about this matter? Learn the truth about your covenant right to healing and divine health and then live well!
BPT 1 (4-CD)

A Lifestyle of Excellence

 Having God's Best is a process of operating in faith and walking godly. If you want to know what is keeping you from receiving God's blessings you need this series to give you the tools to walk in God's prosperity: spirit, soul and body.
BPT 3 (4-CD)

For the latest information on other books, visual and audio products please contact us at:

(800) 927-3436
www.faithdome.org

Faith One Publishing is the publishing arm of Crenshaw Christian Center in Los Angeles, California and publisher of *Ever*  *Increasing Faith Magazine.*

Subscribe or Renew your FREE Magazine Subscription

Website: www.faithdome.org

Call us: (800) 927-3436

This quarterly magazine brings the latest and greatest teachings of Drs. Fred and Betty Price absolutely free to those living in the continental United States. Teachings are geared for the Christian today and cover such areas as:

- ♪ Parenting
- ♪ Health & Healing
- ♪ From the Headlines
- ♪ Testimonies
- ♪ Missions

Keep informed and growing in the things of God by receiving your free copy of this magazine designed to empower you with the Word of Faith.

The Power of Faith to Transform Your Life!

STUDY NOTES

STUDY NOTES

STUDY NOTES